JUMPSTART! WELLBEING

This collection of engaging and simple-to-use activities will help teachers to develop children's mental and emotional wellbeing while also including the thinking skills necessary for learning.

The authors show how developing such skills within the context of a wellbeing agenda aids children's motivation, their ability to concentrate and their willingness to explore, investigate and question, bringing huge benefits for children's sense of achievement, self-confidence and resilience. Drawing on a wealth of practical activities that include both creative and critical ways of thinking, chapters cover:

- wellbeing in the classroom
- emotional resourcefulness
- relaxation and meditation
- mindfulness and reflectiveness
- being well.

Jumpstart! Wellbeing is a treasure trove of fun activities and ideas for building wellbeing and its constituent skills into the curriculum.

Steve Bowkett is a former teacher and the author of numerous books for teachers including the bestselling *Jumpstart! Creativity*. He also works as an Educational Consultant specialising in the areas of thinking skills and problem solving, creativity and literacy.

Kevin Hogston is Head Teacher at Collis Primary School in Teddington, UK. He has worked in primary education for almost 20 years, including the role of an Advanced Skills Teacher for Emotional Wellbeing.

Jumpstart!

JUMPSTART! WELLBEING

GAMES AND ACTIVITIES FOR AGES 7–14

Steve Bowkett and Kevin Hogston

Routledge
Taylor & Francis Group

LONDON AND NEW YORK

First published 2017
by Routledge
2 Park Square, Milton Park, Abingdon, Oxon OX14 4RN

and by Routledge
711 Third Avenue, New York, NY 10017

Routledge is an imprint of the Taylor & Francis Group, an informa business

British Library Cataloguing in Publication Data
A catalogue record for this book is available from the British Library

Library of Congress Cataloging in Publication Data
Names: Bowkett, Stephen, author. | Hogston, Kevin, author.
Title: Jumpstart! wellbeing : games and activities for ages 7-14 / Steve Bowkett and Kevin Hogston.
Description: Abingdon, Oxon ; New York, NY : Routledge, 2017. | Includes bibliographical references.
Identifiers: LCCN 2016013656| ISBN 9781138184015 (hardback) | ISBN 9781138184022 (pbk.) | ISBN 9781315645452 (ebook)
Subjects: LCSH: Students--Mental health. | Well-being--Study and teaching--Activity programs. | Critical thinking--Study and teaching--Activity programs. | Problem solving--Study and teaching--Activity programs. | Activity programs in education.
Classification: LCC LB3430 .B68 2017 | DDC 371.7/13--dc23LC record available at https://lccn.loc.gov/2016013656

ISBN: 978-1-138-18401-5 (hbk)
ISBN: 978-1-138-18402-2 (pbk)
ISBN: 978-1-315-64545-2 (ebk)

Typeset in Palatino and Scala Sans
by Saxon Graphics Ltd, Derby

Contents

List of figures

Acknowledgements

Steve – Again, heartfelt thanks to my friend Tony Hitchman for much of the artwork in this book. I also want to thank my co-author Kevin Hogston both for his enthusiasm and patience during the writing of this book.

Kevin – Many thanks go to Valerie Al-Jawad and Professor Guy Claxton who gave me the inspiration and freedom to do things differently. A special mention to the staff at Collis School for their support, passion and commitment to the Collis children.

Finally, I would like to thank my wife Claire and my family Gracie, Emmeline, mum, dad and Ian for all their wonderful support.

Introduction

Wellbeing might be defined as 'an overarching concept generally held to describe the quality of people's lives'. The concept includes objective and subjective aspects of a person's life such as 'household income, family structure, educational achievement, health status' and an individual's own feelings about these things and their life in general. Wellbeing indicators, especially those used for cross-national comparisons, have tended to focus on objective data: there has been increasing recognition that objective measures of wellbeing are not sufficient for the development of policy, and that subjective indicators based on individuals' self-reports of aspects of life such as happiness, social connectedness, perceived quality of life and life satisfaction are also needed.

Although there are currently no statutory requirements to address the general area of 'wellbeing' in UK schools, most teachers would surely acknowledge that children who are happy, who can deal with stress/anxiety (as an aspect of being more emotionally resourceful) and think creatively as well as analytically are likely not just to be more effective learners but to enjoy their learning more.

The other side of this coin is that children who are stressed and have limited or no strategies for dealing with their negative thoughts and feelings are inhibited in their ability to learn and draw much less enjoyment from the educational process.

How stressed a child is has a direct bearing on how well he/she learns, which in turn affects that child's test results and influences their view of education generally. Ironically SATs themselves are a major cause of stress among children. An article on the BBC News website (www.bbc.co.uk/news/uk-wales-29810114 – 29/10/2014) reported a survey of teachers in Wales which claimed that 'annual school tests for children aged 7 to 14 are causing so much stress some pupils are refusing to go to school'.

Putting 'stress in pupils in UK schools' into a search engine immediately pulls up dozens of references such as the above, each highlighting the widespread nature and degree of stress in pupils of all ages across the country. Interestingly there is also a sprinkling of articles about how different aspects of wellbeing, including relaxation, meditation and 'emotional literacy', are explicitly being addressed in some schools to good effect. The government itself produced a document in June 2014 – *Mental Health and Behaviour in Schools* – where the first of its key findings states that, 'In order to help their pupils succeed, schools have a role to play in supporting them to be resilient and mentally healthy. There are a variety of things that schools can do, for all their pupils and for those with particular problems, to offer that support in an effective way' (Department for Education 2016, p. 6).

The issue of pupil (and teacher) stress and the value of strategies to deal with it have long been recognised. For instance, the Government Office for Science Foresight Report on Mental Capital and Wellbeing (2008) suggests that:

> Wellbeing is a dynamic state that is enhanced when people can fulfil their personal and social goals and achieve a sense of purpose in society. Rather than being static, wellbeing emerges from how people interact with the world around them at different points in their lives. It is not necessarily the same as being happy, since anxiety, depression and anger are sometimes to be expected in life.
>
> (Statham and Chase 2010)

(We would agree with this but add that how someone is able to deal with negative feelings and situations is key to achieving the greatest degree of happiness and fulfilment in one's life.)

Adding weight to this, a Department for Education (DfE) report – *The Impact of Pupil Behaviour and Wellbeing on Educational Outcomes* (DfE 2012a) – included the following among its findings:

- Better emotional wellbeing at age 7 is a significant predictor of higher academic progression from Key Stage 1 to Key Stage 2, although this relationship is not significant at other ages.
- Better attention skills at ages 7, 10, and 13 are a significant predictor of greater academic progression in both primary and secondary school, indicating that the ability to control and sustain attention is a consistent predictor of children's learning.
- Better emotional wellbeing, less troublesome behaviour, fewer activity and attention problems, and more positive friendships at age 10 are associated with greater school engagement from 10 to 13 years, highlighting the significant role of wellbeing in children's engagement as they enter secondary school.
- More school enjoyment at ages 7 and 10 is associated with greater school engagement from ages 7 to 10 and from ages 10 to 13, respectively, indicating that children who enjoy school are more likely to be motivated and engaged in their school work at a later point in time.

Another report reveals these points:

- Children with higher levels of emotional, behavioural, social and school wellbeing, on average, have higher levels of academic achievement and are more engaged in school, both concurrently and in later years.
- Children with better emotional wellbeing make more progress in primary school and are more engaged in secondary school.
- Children with better attention skills experience greater progress across the four key stages of schooling in England. Those who are engaged in less troublesome behaviour also make more progress and are more engaged in secondary school.
- Children who are bullied are less engaged in primary school, whereas those with positive friendships are more engaged in secondary school.
- As children move through the school system, emotional and behavioural wellbeing become more important in explaining

school engagement, while demographic and other characteristics become less important.

- Relationships between emotional, behavioural, social and school wellbeing and later educational outcomes are generally similar for children and adolescents, regardless of their gender and parents' educational level.

(DfE 2012b, pp. 1–2)

Further, the PSHE Association reports on its website that:

> The Government's PSHE education review concluded in March 2013, stating that the subject would remain non-statutory and that no new programmes of study would be published. The DfE has however stated as part of its National Curriculum guidance that, 'All schools should make provision for personal, social, health and economic education (PSHE), drawing on good practice'.

A more recent report (published February 2015) by the House of Commons Education Committee – *Life Lessons: PSHE and SRE in schools* – states that:

> PSHE requires improvement in 40% of schools. The situation appears to have worsened over time, and young people consistently report that the sex and relationships education (SRE) they receive is inadequate. This situation would not be tolerated in other subjects.

The case for incorporating a 'wellbeing programme' into the children's classroom experience is overwhelming, we feel. Our focus in this book will be the mental and emotional aspects of wellbeing (though of course these impact on other areas such as social and physical wellbeing). Our aim is to offer a range of practical and, we hope, effective, strategies, techniques and activities that can easily be built in to your day-to-day running of the classroom.

HOW TO USE THE BOOK

Many of the activities can be used by themselves, for instance as lesson starters to help children get into the mood for learning. Some lend themselves more to discussion, reflection and subsequent writing, and so would form the main focus of a lesson. Where appropriate we have explained how you can extend activities, both by increasing the challenge to children's thinking and by cross-referencing with other exercises. The 'dip in' nature of the book means that some activities appear in more than one section, though we have tried to offer different variations of the techniques where this occurs.

The activities across the different chapters complement and reinforce each other and are loosely sequenced through the five chapters, thus they can offer a progression that leads children towards a greater understanding of wellbeing and how to achieve it in their lives, both within and beyond school.

CHAPTER 1

Jumpstart wellbeing in the classroom

> Work on yourself and serve the world.
>
> (Traditional Arabic saying)

This section features some quick and easy activities that you can build into the children's day, and which pave the way for the higher-challenge yet more powerful techniques you'll find in the subsequent sections.

MEMORY AND IMAGINATION

Two important points to note at the outset are, first, that we all possess the vital resources of memory and imagination. 'Memory' here is not being used in the same sense as recall. To recall is to 'call back again' into conscious awareness previous thoughts and feelings in the form of memories. We often do this deliberately, as when we choose to think about a holiday that we have enjoyed, a good time we had with friends or some particular achievement that gave us pleasure. Notice that the thoughts and feelings that constitute a memory are fully entwined: it's difficult if not impossible to think about a past event without the accompanying feelings and attendant physiological reactions.

Memory used in the broader sense means the sum total of our experiences and the associations we have made between them. Much of this material exists at a subconscious level, but is nonetheless active in shaping our attitudes, beliefs and consequent behaviours. This astonishingly complex network of memories is sometimes called the 'map of reality', yet like any map it is not the real thing but rather a representation of the sense that each of us has made of the world, based on our (conscious and subconscious) interpretation of events. Thus our individual map, while having many things in common with other people's, is still highly subjective and individual.

Sometimes memories come to mind unbidden, spontaneously. This might be because something happening at the present moment triggers an association that 'lifts' the memory into conscious awareness. Such a recollection might be pleasant or unpleasant. Negative memories that keep coming back can represent 'unfinished business' or issues that have not yet been resolved. When these are deeply troubling then specialist help is recommended, but less serious negative thoughts-and-feelings can often be dealt with successfully by using the techniques we explain in this book. The crucial point is that once a memory has become conscious it can be noticed, reflected upon, reappraised and modified as necessary in order to make it more useful to us, insofar as it adds to a sense of wellbeing rather than detracts from it.

Imagination is the ability we have to create mental scenarios that need have nothing to do with our immediate circumstances. We can imagine things (using the resource of memory, as defined above) to visualise a future that hasn't happened yet and, indeed, to experience in our minds things that are in reality impossible. By the same token we can envisage things that are possible and that we desire to achieve. As the saying goes; before the action comes the vision.

The second key point is that the resources of memory and imagination can be more fully utilised by cultivating the behaviours of noticing and questioning. Encouraging children to do these more actively and deliberately will enhance the effectiveness of the wellbeing techniques below and, indeed, children's more general ability to learn.

But enough of the theory. Let's get stuck in to some practical activities…

OUTSIDE WORLD, INSIDE WORLD

The 'common sense' view of reality is that my sense of self – my conscious mind – exists inside my head while the world at large lies 'out there' and consists of everything else. There are all kinds of philosophical implications to this idea (which unfortunately we don't have space to explore), but it will serve as a working model for helping children to develop a greater sense of wellbeing.

A powerful tendency in many if not all people is to perceive the world through the filter of our values and beliefs. This can be summed up by saying that 'perception is projection': we see and interpret things according to the way we think and feel, which we then 'project' back on to the world such that our ongoing view is confirmed. As the old saying goes, an angry man lives in an angry world. This principle applies both to short-term moods and more entrenched and ongoing attitudes. An important aspect of developing mental and emotional wellbeing is to recognise the perception-is-projection process as a precursor to doing something about it.

- The World Inside. Show the class the image in Figure 1.1 and say, 'This is what's going on in the mind of someone of about your age. Firstly, what do you notice in the picture? Why might he (or she) be thinking about these things? And why might he be thinking about them *in this way*?'

Point out to the children that there isn't necessarily a right answer to these questions. Their interpretations are all equally valid. Take the children's ideas one at a time and follow up with the question, 'So if he's looking at things in that way, how do you think it makes him feel?' This reinforces the notion that 'We don't see things as they are, we see them as we are' (Anais Nin).

If an interpretation of the images in the circle results in the character feeling good, ask the class how they would redraw the images to make the character feel even better. Similarly, if a child says that the character would feel angry, sad, etc., by imagining the images in a certain way, ask how they could be changed to turn negative feelings into more positive ones.

3

Figure 1.1 The world inside

Extend the activity by asking the children what they would put into a circle to create a chosen positive feeling.

This very simple and straightforward task can lead to some useful and searching discussions. For instance, a child might say he would put bars of chocolate into the circle to create a feeling of happiness. Explore this further with the class by asking questions such as these:

– How long might such happiness last?
– Would the chocolate make lots of people feel happy? Most people? All people?

- Does happiness always depend on physical things?
- What else can make people happy?

- A more sophisticated version of the circle game uses a template like the one in Figure 1.2. Again, the large circle represents a person's conscious mind, while the other circles represent things that the character is thinking about.

  The size of the subsidiary circles indicates their importance to the person concerned. Overlapping circles mean that whatever they represent are linked in some way. Circles that protrude beyond the edge of the large circle are being outwardly expressed in some way.

  Split the class into groups and ask each group to label the subsidiary circles – in other words, to suggest what's on the character's mind. Again there is no single right answer to this task.

- Extend the activity by making sets of circles out of thin card. Children in groups or individually can then move circles around to alter the mental-emotional landscape of the character. The benefits of this activity include the following:

  - Helping children to make links between different emotions.
  - Becoming more familiar with a greater range of emotions.
  - Sowing the seeds of the idea that emotions are not fixed and unchanging.
  - Reinforcing the notion that feelings can be changed by deliberate, conscious interventions.

Literacy link: Both of the circle-based activities above can be used to help children to create more well-rounded characters in their stories.

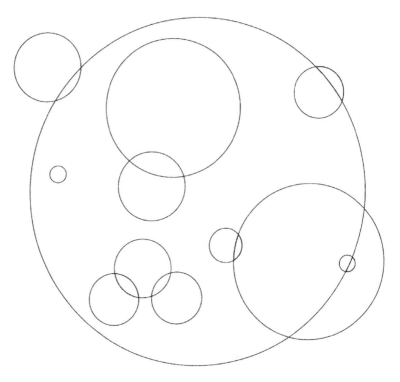

Figure 1.2 Circle game

BE NOSY AND NOTICE SOMETHING

Children are often asked to 'pay attention' without necessarily being shown how to develop that skill. Here are some ideas for you to try out.

- Ask the children to look around the classroom to notice something they have either not noticed before or not noticed for a long time.
- Assemble a tray of small objects and make one change each day; add something, take something away, swap something. Challenge the children to spot what you've done. Increase the difficulty of the task by increasing the number of objects in the

tray and make two or three changes each day. This is the classic Kim's game.

- Encourage the children to notice something positive about a classmate and, as appropriate, pay them a compliment.
- Type 'images of objects hidden in pictures' into your search engine. There are hundreds of such pictures that can be downloaded to help develop the children's observational skills.
- Invite the children to keep a notebook of interesting things they notice at school, home and in the area.
- One unique detail. Ask children to notice something about an object that makes it different from others of its kind. Extend the activity by inviting the children to notice one unique detail about a classmate that reflects something positive about them, either in terms of appearance or personality.
- Get the children to work in pairs. Give each pair two similar items – two stones, flowers, leaves, coins, etc. – and ask them to notice as many differences between these things as they can.

Literacy link: Show the class two almost identical sentences and ask them to point out the difference or differences.

For example:

> I took a book from my brother's bookcase.
> I took a book from my brothers' bookcase.

It's not necessary for children to understand the use of the possessive apostrophe in this case (though you can explain or revisit if you wish). What matters is that they are encouraged to notice the subtle difference. Extend the activity by showing the class two almost identical pieces of text and inviting them to spot the differences. Subsequently, ask the children to create examples of their own. This helps to develop editing skills as well as concentration.

- Ask the children to sit quietly with their bodies relaxed. Show them a small object such as a tennis ball. Explain that their *point of attention* is now fixed on the ball. After half a minute or so, ask them to 'defocus' their attention and, still watching the ball (i.e. without looking round), to become aware of the room around them. You can suggest that they feel even more relaxed and settled as they do this. Just sitting quietly, doing nothing in this way, acts as a precursor to the relaxation/meditation techniques explained in Chapter 3.

This simple activity creates the opportunity for you to explain the notion of peripheral vision. This idea in turn serves as an analogy to help the children to understand that while certain thoughts (and accompanying feelings) can be in the forefront of the mind, so others exist more at the edges of our attention. So, for instance, we can feel a little anxious about something without really noticing that we are, although that 'background' emotion can still be having a negative effect on our general outlook as well as influencing our current mood. Noticing the feeling – pointing the conscious attention towards it – is the first step in dealing with it effectively.

OBSERVATIONS OF NATURE WITHOUT JUDGEMENT

Another tendency in the way many people think is to attach a judgement (involving an emotional response) to an observation. This may be done unthinkingly – a kind of mental knee-jerk reflex – or reflect an ongoing attitude that might be consciously and deliberately cultivated.

This mode of thinking has been called an 'obserpinion'; an observation glued to an opinion. When this becomes a habit such thoughts can generalise out and attract a powerful emotional charge. See the section on generalising in Chapter 2 (p. 50) for more on this. Negative obserpinions applied to groups can have detrimental consequences for all concerned. In the two weeks prior to writing this, Steve met somebody who 'hates the French', another person who feels that BMW drivers 'are all stupid idiots' and a third who believes that 'teenagers are lazy'. (At this point notice if you have just experienced any immediate and unbidden emotional response to these statements.)

Obserpinions of this kind are often expressed using extreme language and may well not be supported by any strong evidence.

Such evidence where it does exist might be mere hearsay, gleaned from newspapers or the opinions of others, or perhaps based on a small number of experiences that have been interpreted so as to support an already-existing view.

In helping children to avoid generalising in this way, or to enable them to examine (and hopefully modify) negative opinions they already hold, look at the natural world first, this being a more neutral arena for thinking than discussing different groups of people.

- Ask the class to see how many personifications of the weather they can find; also examples of how we sometimes use exaggerated language to talk about it… It's a filthy day / foul weather / stinking wind and rain / disgusting snow and ice / appalling weather conditions / scorching day / lashing down with rain / I'm freezing my socks off out here, etc.
- Show the class pictures of animals and ask the children about their emotional reactions to them – cuddly lion cubs and tamarin monkeys vs tangles of snakes and swarms of ants. The aim here is simply to *notice* how quickly and automatically an emotional response can follow the image of the animal.
- Invite the children to write down short and simple descriptions of the natural world (ideally of things they experience directly themselves), choosing their words carefully to avoid exaggeration, personification or overblown language. So 'The cold wind came in gusts that made the leaves quiver and hiss' rather than 'The freezing wind howled and screamed through the trees and nearly blew me off my feet'.

The educational benefits of encouraging the writing of such descriptions include the following:

- Helping to focus attention on small details.
- Developing curiosity.
- Refining the senses.
- Improving vocabulary.
- Highlighting the importance of word choice linked with the purpose of the writing.

- Developing appreciation of the natural world and, more broadly, an aesthetic sense.
- Paving the way to an understanding of the interdependency of all things and the fact that life is a process; a flowing rather than a series of discrete events.

Literacy link: An activity that many children enjoy is writing a simplified form of haiku poem. (Steve calls this 'myku' poetry – my kind of haiku.) The syllabic structure is 2, 3, 4 over three lines. One attraction of the activity is that it involves very little writing (!) but plenty of thinking to choose words carefully so that every word does some work. Here are examples of nature myku from Year 5 and Year 6 pupils.

Gate bolt
so restless –
Rattling wind.

Just this –
butterfly,
a sunny wall.

Today –
one more grain
in the sand clock.

No moon.
What shadow's
behind the wall?

Pebbles,
pink, grey, white –
They're all pebbles.

A bee
to and fro –
going somewhere?

Apples
don't think but
get on with it!

All of these examples can be summed up by the philosopher Alfred North Whitehead's cautionary advice that 'we think in generalities, but we live in detail'.

APPRECIATION

The word itself comes from the Latin verb *appretiare*, meaning 'to appraise' or 'to set a price' and nowadays means to value, cherish, respect, admire or more fully understand something or someone. Cultivating a deeper sense of appreciation involves exploring things in more detail, refining the sensibilities and being able to look at the world with a different perspective (this last being a key feature of creative thinking).

- Start simply by asking the class to think about and discuss subtle differences between things. Take synonyms as an example. How would the children explain the difference between little and small, bright and brilliant, instruct and train, etc.? (One way of doing this is to look at the etymology of the words, though more immediately the purpose is to challenge children to try to explain the distinction in their own words.)

  Extend the activity by utilising the other senses. Get the children to listen to similar sounds and try to explain how they are different. Ask them to smell different spices – how would they describe the smell of cardamom seeds, a cinnamon stick, fennel seeds…? How does cotton cloth feel different from wool, and wool from silk? Point out that a child's reaction to the smell is different from an attempt to describe the smell itself: 'It's a nice smell' as distinct from 'It's a sweet smell that reminds me of roses'.

- Offer the children a 'WOW [World of Wonder] fact' of the day. Hundreds of these can be found online, while the *Guinness Book of Records* is another great source of information. Invite children to find an astonishing did-you-know fact themselves and present it to the class. These can be linked to a current topic or area of study.

Did you know?

- There are more stars in the universe than grains of sand in all the beaches in the world.
- The total weight of all the ants on Earth is greater than the weight of all humans.
- Archaeologists have found 2,000-year-old jars of honey in Egyptian tombs that still tasted delicious.
- There are six million parts in the Boeing 747-400 aeroplane.
- No piece of paper can be folded in half more than seven times (here's one you can try at home).
- Ostriches can run faster than horses and male ostriches can roar like lions.

- In Your Shoes. Any activity that invites children to imagine what the world looks like from someone else's perspective helps to develop an important element of appreciation and empathy. This can take many forms. Asking children to talk about their hobbies and interests is a good start. Consider inviting people from different backgrounds into school to talk to the children about their own particular challenges, difficulties, achievements and plans.
- Recognising small acts of kindness demonstrates appreciation. This amounts to more than good manners and politeness. A sincere thank you or 'I appreciate that' contributes to the social cohesion of a group and helps to build friendships.
- A further, and very important, aspect of appreciation is to 'be here now'; to appreciate the fact of one's own existence in the moment. We deal with this more fully in Chapter 4.

CATEGORISING THOUGHTS

The ability to notice and modify one's own thoughts is known as metacognition, literally 'thinking about thinking'. An early step towards building this key skill is to ask the class to categorise their thoughts. This does not necessarily mean that children need to tell each other what they are thinking about, and they certainly don't need to reveal any personal information. You can set up the activity by saying, 'Imagine we have some boxes and each box will contain different kinds of thoughts. What labels could we put on the boxes?'

There are no set answers to this question and any number of boxes is acceptable. The activity will start off as more of a brainstorming session, though once you have collected a good stock of ideas you can ask the children to reflect on them further...

- Sometimes children will say the same things in different ways. 'Nice thoughts' and 'pleasant thoughts' mean the same thing. Point out that this would form one category rather than two.
- Encourage the children to explore subtle distinctions. Are 'pleasant thoughts' and 'happy thoughts' identical ideas? How could a thought be pleasant yet not make you feel happy?
- Explore the size of different categories of thoughts. Thoughts about the past and thoughts about the future could be considered sub-categories of thoughts about time. See 'nested hierarchies' on the next page.
- Get the children to think metaphorically about thoughts. An 'association web' is a common example, as is a 'train' of thought. In what sense are thoughts like a web or a train? Offer children further examples and/or ask them to make up their own. What kind of thoughts would be cloud thoughts, lightning thoughts, river thoughts, butterfly thoughts, etc.? Another way of tackling this activity is to say 'Thoughts are sometimes like clouds because...?'

NESTED HIERARCHIES

This is the where smaller categories are placed within larger groups, as illustrated in Figure 1.3. In this case four categories are 'nested' together, like four Russian dolls one inside the other, inside the other... If you feel that this will confuse children, cut down on the number of categories and/or give a few examples to illustrate the idea. 'Each of you would fit inside the bigger group that we call this class, which would fit inside the bigger group of Year 6 (let's say), which fits inside the even bigger group of KS2, which fits inside the bigger group of this whole school.'

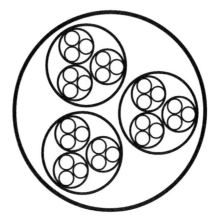

Figure 1.3 Nested hierarchies

Ask the children to review all the examples of thoughts they have given to see if they can create any nested hierarchies.

Develop this way of thinking by asking the class to create nested hierarchies within given themes. Offer an example first that fits the diagram – so, lion, tiger, cheetah / cats / mammals / animals. Or Monday, Tuesday, Wednesday / week / month / year.

- Infoscraps. These are simply scraps of paper with ideas – in this case categories of thoughts – written on them. Sets of infoscraps are accompanied by a question or an instruction – for example, 'Arrange the scraps in order of how often you think these kinds of thoughts' or 'Put the scraps in order of how important you think these kinds of thoughts are'.

Explain that the infoscraps don't necessarily need to be arranged in a straight line. If two categories are considered to be equally important they will be placed side by side.

Note also that because the categories do not consist of actual examples of thoughts, children can work with the category 'unpleasant thoughts' without needing to remember any.

For more uses of infoscraps see Steve's book *Jumpstart Thinking Skills and Problem Solving* (Bowkett 2015).

UNIQUENESS

The word 'unique' derives from the Latin *unus* meaning 'one' and thence from *unicus* meaning 'only, single, one of its kind'. Helping children to appreciate the uniqueness of people, places and things cultivates a sense of wonder in the complexity and diversity of the world; while encouraging them to realise their *own* uniqueness develops respect for others and a heightened sense of self-respect (using the word respect here in the sense of 'looking back' or 'looking again' to discover something new).

We have already touched on the notion of uniqueness in the section 'Be nosy and notice something' (p. 6). Extend this work now by trying the following activities.

> Today will never happen again.
> (Og Mandino, American author)

- Uniqueness of the present moment. The image of the hourglass is a powerful metaphor to help us realise the inexorable nature of time passing. The sand grains that have already passed through the waist of the hourglass can never be recovered: the single grain passing through *now* is the only one over which we have any direct influence. The decisions and choices we make in the present moment can obviously affect what we do in the future, with the proviso that ultimately the future is uncertain. This realisation itself can be used to reflect on the importance of what we do now, how we use our time, wherein lies our only power (reference: *The Power of Now* by Eckhart Tolle (2005), see Bibliography).

Another metaphor for time is money. We spend time, try to save it or buy it and sometimes we waste it. In today's culture we even maintain that time *is* money. (This idea would form the basis of an interesting class discussion on values.)

Ask children if they know or can think of any other metaphors for time. Tell the class about the arrow of time (an important idea in modern cosmology) or the notion that time flows like a river. We commonly use the metaphor of space when talking about time, as in phrases like 'the distant past, 'the far future', 'a long time', etc. Useful sources of such comparisons, plus other relevant quotes, can be found at www.metaphorsandsimiles.com and http://grammar.about.com.

If you feel that the children will understand the idea, you can also talk to them about the spirit of the times (the so-called *zeitgeist*). What is it that helps to characterise a certain period in history? What does it mean to say that something was 'of its time'? What does 'a sign of the times' mean?

- The uniqueness of place. Locations too can have their own special mood or atmosphere.

- Ask children about their favourite places and why they are so special. How does being in this place make you feel?

- Show the class pictures of different locations around the world and ask the children to reflect on their uniqueness.

- Use nature poetry to help children appreciate the qualities of particular places and times.

The Victorian poet Gerard Manley Hopkins felt that everything in existence possessed its own individual identity, an idea he termed inscape. He also believed that such identity was not a static thing but a process: everything expresses its uniqueness dynamically – as Hopkins says, things 'selve', they 'go themselves'. (The same concept was recognised by the American inventor and architect Buckminster Fuller when he famously said 'I seem to be a verb'.) Human beings can appreciate the inscape of things, an act that Hopkins called instress, which he strove to demonstrate in much of his poetry. While the poems themselves can be difficult, Hopkins' nature journals are full of beautiful and powerful descriptions of nature that many children will find to be accessible.

Tip: 'Myku' poems are a useful way for children to try to capture the special qualities of a place or occasion. See 'Observations of nature without judgement' in this chapter (p. 8).

I-DENTITY

Appreciating our own uniqueness helps to enhance our sense of identity. But what exactly do we mean by that? How do we explore who we are?

- Ask the children to think about the language we use when speaking about ourselves. We talk about 'my arms, my legs' as though these things belonged to me but were not *me*; as though 'I' am distinct from my body, although of course my body contributes to my sense of identity.

Challenge the class with this philosophical thought experiment... If a person lost an arm in an accident and had it replaced by an artificial limb, would he or she still *essentially* be the same person? (What do we mean by 'essence' anyway?) What if artificial limbs and organs replaced 50 per cent of his body – would he then have only half of his identity or would he essentially be the same person? What if his mind could be stored in a computer with all of his memories and other thoughts complete and intact? Would he still be the same personality that he was before?

What if, once this (unfortunate) person's mind was stored in a computer, one thought was deleted? Would his personality be a little bit less than it was before? Would he be something less than he was? What if one thought each day was deleted; would his personality shrink and shrink until it was no longer there? At what point would his personality disappear, do you think?

What if the person's mind (in his original brain or in a computer) could be *added to*? In other words, what if someone else's thoughts could be implanted without the person's knowledge into his mind; would be become more of a personality, a split personality, a different personality?

What if artificial intelligence (AI) actually happened – would the AI computer have a personality?

- Explore the origins of the words we use when talking about who we think we are. Here are some examples.

  - Individual – from the Latin meaning 'not able to be divided' (as in indivisible).
  - Person – again from the Latin; persona, 'an actor's mask, a character in a play' (suggesting that the 'real' person lay behind the mask).
  - Identity – from the sixteenth century meaning 'the quality of being the same', and further back from the Latin idem meaning 'same'. How can we equate this definition with the usual modern meaning of the word? (Our own thought on this is that it's to do with 'continuity of consciousness'. We feel we are the same person even though the personality matures and the body ages.)
  - I – from the Greek *ego* (ego itself being a term used in psychology meaning 'the self').
  - Memory – from the Latin *memor*, 'mindful, remembering'. (To continue with the thought experiment above, if there are some

memories in my mind that I can never remember, and if these hidden memories were deleted, would I be the same person? Would I think I was?)

- Thought – from Old English meaning 'process of thinking' and 'compassion', in the sense of 'to conceive of in the mind; to consider'. The modern definition of 'compassion' by the way is 'pity, inclining one to spare or help' (*Concise Oxford Dictionary*) due to 'feeling with' someone in their suffering.

ALL TOGETHER NOW

While we can and should celebrate our uniqueness and individuality, and try to appreciate these in others, it's important to recognise that our lives are inextricably linked to other huge networks of people, places and processes; sometimes obviously but often in very subtle ways that take some reflection to realise.

It was the English novelist E. M. Forster who said 'Only connect… Live in fragments no longer.' While his context was connecting 'the prose and the passion', the principle of his wisdom applies more widely. Further, making new links in our minds is one of the key elements of creative thinking – taking two or more previously separate ideas and forging a connection to make something new and something more. Actively connecting in this way generates information – in-formation, the forming of greater meanings and understandings in our imagination. Any activity that utilises the principle of linking (and looking at something in a different way) is per se a creative process.

Here are some ideas to develop children's ability in this field.

- Linking game. Split the illustration in Figure 1.4 into its three sections and show them separately to the class.

  As the children look at the pictures-only section say, 'Pick any two images and tell me a link between them.' Point out that there can be a number of connections between any two images chosen and that, again, there is no one right answer to the task.

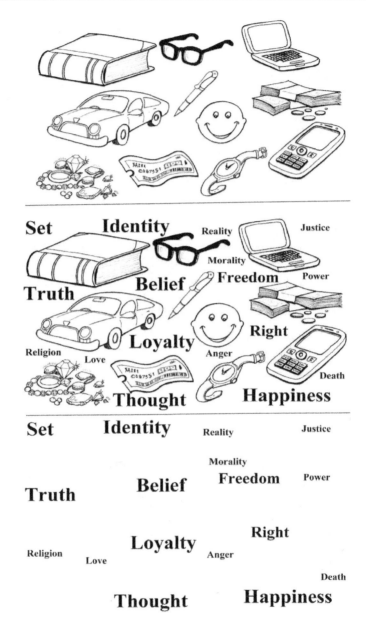

Figure 1.4 Linking game

A variation of the game is for you to pick two items and ask the class collectively to come up with as many ways of linking them as they can. Further challenge the children by picking three or more images and asking for links between them.

The middle section adds concepts to the images. These concepts are often ones used to generate philosophical discussions. Say, 'Now I want you to pick any two of the pictures (you can use ones you've chosen earlier) plus one of the words and tell me a link between all three.' As a precursor to this stage of the game, you might want to explore the meanings of certain of the words if some children aren't sure of them.

Literacy link: Both sections can be used to create 'seed stories', brief and simple ideas that can be developed into stories later. Say, 'Choose two images from the selection. If you were going to use both of them in a story, what would the story basically be about? Try to tell me in one sentence.'

Adding a concept word to the task gives the potential narrative a theme; an underpinning idea that will make the story more cohesive. So in the pictures-only version a child might reply, 'I choose the jewels and the fast car. A man steals some jewels and makes his getaway in a fast car.' Adding the underpinning concept you might get, 'Because he has felt trapped in poverty and thinks that lots of money will give him freedom.'

You can see that this is a richer and more robust idea that gives the character's motives a powerful (if misguided) reason for his actions. It also forms the basis of a potentially valuable discussion on the morality of what the man does.

Using the concept words by themselves makes the activity more abstract and more difficult. Again ask children to pick two concept words (or choose for them) and forge a link between them. How might belief and identity be linked, or truth and anger?

Tip: If you decide to use one or more of these broad concepts as the basis for a discussion, children are often helped if the idea is broken down into a number of smaller-scale questions – as below.

- What do we mean by truth?
- Is it always right to tell the truth?
- How can we know if something is true? (Give some examples with proofs of truth.)
- What are some reasons for people deciding not to tell the truth?
- Would you rather tell a small lie to avoid hurting someone's feelings, or stick strictly to the principle of always telling the truth?

- Chicken stir-fry. The title of this activity is just one of hundreds of examples. In this case, itemise the ingredients for the children (including the kitchen equipment used) and ask them to find out where these things came from. When one class tried this in a workshop with Steve, they were amazed that over a dozen different countries were involved. The class then made a display using pictures and lengths of wool to show how all of the ingredients 'converged' on Britain so that the stir-fry dish could be made.
- Take an everyday item such as a tea bag and trace it back to its origins. Someone put the box of tea bags on the supermarket shelf. Someone delivered the box from the warehouse to the store. Someone brought the box of tea bags from the factory to the warehouse, etc. Eventually we arrive at the person who picked the raw tea leaves in some distant part of the world.
- Take a complex system such as a town, a living organism, a school, etc., and explore how all these parts contribute to the workings of the whole. (This can lead to discussion on how, sometimes, the whole can be more than the sum of the parts – see for example the sections on uniqueness and I-dentity (pp. 15 and 17).

SLOW DOWN

The so-called 'Slow Movement' began in 1986 when Carlo Petrini protested against the opening of a fast-food outlet in his home city of Rome. The core principle of the Slow Movement is to encourage a cultural shift towards altering what is seen as the frenetic pace of life in many areas of modern living. An influential contribution to the cause came with the publication of Carl Honoré's book *In Praise of Slow* (2004), in which the author is clear to point out that he does not advocate people doing everything at a snail's pace, but doing things at the right speed, taking time to savour an experience while realising that faster is not necessarily better.

In his book Honoré quotes Kathy Hirsh-Pasek, a Professor of psychology, who co-authored *Einstein Never Used Flash Cards: how children really learn – and why they need to play more and memorize less* (Hirsh-Pasek and Golinkoff 2004). Hirsh-Pasek is quoted as stating that scientific evidence suggests that children learn more effectively and develop more rounded personalities when they learn in a more relaxed, less regimented and less hurried way. Accepting this creates a dilemma of course in the current educational climate where the imperative is on coverage of a content-laden curriculum. (The educationalist John Abbott, president of The 21st Century Learning Initiative [www.21learn.org] sums this up very forcefully in asserting that the curriculum is half a mile wide but only half an inch deep.)

It is hardly controversial to suggest that things are best done at their *right* pace, whatever that may be, and that some activities bring most benefits when undertaken slowly and reflectively. Additionally, showing children how to slow down aids concentration, helps to develop observational and other attentional skills and prepares them to master the various relaxation techniques explained later in this book.

Designate a certain part of the school day as 'slow time'. During this period, which need only be 5 or 10 minutes long, give the children something to do where a leisurely pace enhances the experience.

- You might ask them each to bring an interesting object into school – a shell, a paperweight, a picture – to show to a friend, who takes time to examine the item and then talks about what he has noticed.
- Ask the children to relax and play them a quiet and slow-paced piece of music.
- Slowly read an extract from a story, or a piece of descriptive writing, taking time to savour the sound of the language. Some poems too are deliberately written to be read slowly and, indeed, can be understood more readily when you do this. Keats' 'Ode to Autumn' is a perfect example. If you use it, point out to the children that it's not important if they don't understand some parts of it; what matters is that they notice the lulling cadence of the lines.
- Slow eating. Ask each child to bring in a piece of fruit (or something equally healthy!) and spend their slow time eating it. Encourage them to notice the texture of the food and its smell as well as its taste. Ask them to chew the food slowly and make sure it is properly chewed before swallowing.
- On a pleasant day, take the children outside. Ask them to sit quietly and just listen to the sounds around them. Ask them to notice the breeze and, if the weather is right, the slow drift of clouds across the sky.
- Take the children on a walk, either outside or around the school, but have them walk at half speed. Ask them to notice at least three things during the walk that they have not noticed before.

NOTICING MYSELF

How often have you seen someone, in a café perhaps, fidgeting as they talked with a friend; picking at a finger nail, jigging a knee, fiddling with a spoon or whatever? This is often being done quite unconsciously and seems to be the outward expression of what has been called 'nervous tension'. Such a state indicates that the person is not fully *here now*; not completely aware of him or herself and possibly not paying full attention to what the friend is saying. It's easy of course, when you have something on your mind, for niggling thoughts to be very distracting. But allowing yourself to be distracted can detract from the fullness and enjoyment of the present moment. Aside from that, being distracted by such thoughts is not the same as applying strategies for resolving whatever issues they represent.

Learning to become more self-aware and to focus attention in the present moment is a subtle skill. We habitually divide our attention between the 'outside world' and the thoughts that stream continuously through our minds – the philosopher Colin Wilson said that most people live 90 per cent of their lives in their heads. Making a small effort to address this habit and deliberately seek to change it enhances our self-control and paves the way to learn the more powerful techniques we look at later.

- Irish people use the phrase 'catch yourself on' to mean becoming more aware of a problem or situation. A very easy task is to ask children simply to notice themselves. Are they doing any of that nervy knee jigging or nail picking? Ask them to choose to stop it (even if a minute later they have started again). Show them how to do a quick stress check – smooth out a frown, relax hunched shoulders and stomach muscles if these are tightened. This takes just seconds. Encourage children to practise regularly, perhaps by having a poster on the wall to remind them.
- Idle vs deliberate daydreaming. Often, when you notice someone daydreaming and say 'a penny for your thoughts' they can't tell you much about them: the thoughts were hardly being noticed. The daydreams were idle in the same way that an engine when idling isn't doing any useful work. Begin to teach the children to daydream deliberately. Ask them to count mentally to ten, or to go through the alphabet, seeing and/or hearing each digit or letter in their imagination as they do so. Ask them to do a mental tour of the school, or to visualise the classroom and where their classmates are sitting. This will help them to master the more sophisticated visualisations we look at later.
- Stand back. It's easy to get caught up in the moment, which is fine if the situation is pleasant and enjoyable. During a disagreement or quarrel, however, to be tangled up in it can cause things to escalate and allow feelings of anger or upset to dominate. Ask the children to imagine two people arguing (these

can be imaginary characters) while they 'stand back' mentally and watch it happening. When they can do this easily, ask them to recall a real argument they were involved in and again to stand back and look upon this as a more detached observer. Encourage the children to notice any feelings that come up and to say to themselves, 'I notice that feeling of anger, frustration, etc.'. (We'll look at some techniques for changing unhelpful feelings in due course.)

PHYSICAL WARMUP

Because the mind and the body are fundamentally linked, relaxing physically has a beneficial effect on calming thoughts and reducing feelings of tension. You may already practise a physical warmup routine with the children as a way of getting them into 'learning mode'; here are some further suggestions.

Full breath
Stand with feet together and body relaxed. Exhale deeply. As you slowly inhale (through the nose ideally) push out the stomach for a moment then draw the stomach in and let the chest expand. Also rise up on your toes. As you begin to do this, mentally start to count to ten and bring your arms up from the side so that your hands meet over your head as you reach ten.

Now slowly reverse the process, lowering your arms and exhaling to a count of ten.

Side bend
Stand up straight with feet apart. Raise arms at the side to shoulder height, palms facing downward. Slowly bend at the waist to the left. Slowly bring the right arm overhead and slide your left hand down the left leg. Keep your neck relaxed. Then slowly straighten up to your original position and repeat the bend on the right side.

Stand and twist
Stand straight but relaxed, feet together. Slowly raise your arms out in front of you to shoulder level, palms facing downward. Slowly

twist arms and trunk 90 degrees to the left. Do not move your legs or feet. Hold this position for a moment then return to the frontward position before repeating the twist on the right side.

Hip bend

Stand up straight with feet together. Lift your arms overhead so that they are parallel with palms facing each other. Keep your knees straight and slowly bend to the left, still keeping your arms parallel. Hold this position for a moment then slowly straighten up before repeating the bend on the right side.

Eye exercise

Look straight ahead. Without moving your head, roll your eyes upward and hold for a second. Now roll your eyes in a circle; to the right, downwards, to the left, upwards again, then look straight ahead. Repeat by rolling eyes anti-clockwise.

Neck roll

Keep your shoulders relaxed. Slowly bend your head forward until your chin touches your chest. Slowly roll and twist your head to the right (do not hunch your shoulders). Then roll and twist head backwards, then to the left and then round to the front again. Repeat the roll-twist in the opposite direction.

Notes for the teacher

All of these movements should be done slowly and gently. They are most beneficial if repeated about five times, though some children may prefer to do fewer repetitions or not do the exercises at all, which is fine. Similarly, if any children do not want to try these exercises for whatever reason they should be allowed to sit out.

POISED POSTURE

Paying attention to posture while sitting or kneeling is physically beneficial in itself. It also develops concentration and self-awareness and aids meditation practice, as we explain later. The instructions to give to the class are on the next page.

- Simple good sitting.

Sit upright, ideally on a straight-backed chair with your feet flat on the floor. Rest your hands on your thighs, palms downward; or have your hands cupped in your lap. Slowly bend forwards and back a few times, then slowly and gently rock from side to side. This will help you to find your 'centre' and most comfortable sitting position.

Do a 'relaxation check'. Make sure that your shoulders are not hunched and that you are not frowning. Your head should be in line with your spine. Look straight ahead. The aim is to feel poised, yet balanced and relaxed. Enjoy simple good sitting for a minute or two, even if you are not doing it for any other reason.

- Floor sitting.

Using a cushion or mat if necessary, sit on the floor cross-legged with the knees as close to the floor as possible without straining. Sit upright; not rigidly but in a poised way with shoulders relaxed. You can rest your hands on your thighs, palms downwards, or cupped in your lap. Look straight ahead. If you maintain this position for more than a few minutes, cross your ankles the other way round.

Tip: Resting your hands on your knees will gently stretch your thigh and groin muscles.

- Kneeling.

You may prefer a kneeling position rather than sitting. Use a padded mat if possible for greater comfort. Keep your knees together and gently ease back so that your bottom is resting on your feet. Keep your back straight; poised but not rigid. Your head should be in line with your spine. You can rest your hands, palms downward, on your thighs or knees, or cupped in your lap.

Tip: If you find that it's uncomfortable to stay in this position for long, try placing a small cushion under your bottom and between your ankles.

JUST LISTENING

Simply listening while in a quiet frame of mind, without analysing or judging, can be extremely calming. Attention might be focused on a particular sound, or the mind may be relaxed so that sounds wash over while you let them come and go. Here are some quick and easy listening activities, written as you might instruct the children

- Sitting quietly, just listen to the sound of your own breathing. Breathe through your nose if possible. There's no need to try to breathe any differently than you normally do. To enjoy the activity even more, tell yourself that you will become more and more relaxed with every breath you take.
- Listen to the various sounds you can hear from where you're sitting. Perhaps you can hear small noises in the classroom; someone shuffling, a yawn, a sneeze... Maybe you can hear the sound of the wind blowing by outside, or traffic, an aeroplane, people talking, children playing... After a little while, focus your attention on the quietest sound you can hear.

To extend the activity, ask children to pay attention to particular aspects of sound such as volume, pitch, tone, direction, continuous or intermittent, etc. You might say, 'Now try to listen out for something making a long drawn-out sound... Now listen to a sound that's coming from your left... now your right', etc.

- Tibetan singing bowls make a beautiful and deeply calming sound. Each bowl we've heard has its own individual tone. You can make the bowl 'sing' by tapping the beater against the vessel and also by rubbing it around the bowl's rim. A beater is a length of wood that may or may not be covered in leather: if so covered the musical note is much softer. The relaxing effect of the slowly fading note is more pronounced we've found if the bowl is held close to the ear.
- Invite the children to listen to sounds within their own imagination. Ask them to imagine, say, the sound of a stream and hold it in their mind for a specified time. Begin with short periods of concentration, for instance 10 seconds, gradually extending the length each time you run the activity. Ask children

to come up with ideas for sounds that their classmates and you will find pleasing.

NOTICING THE BREATH

It's become a movie cliché that when someone is in a dramatic situation a well-meaning friend encourages them to 'just breathe'. In fact that's good advice. Breathing is one of those physical functions that, like blinking, usually happens automatically but can be brought under conscious control. And because the mind and body are linked, deliberately slowing the pace of breathing has a calming effect on one's thoughts and then potentially on unhelpful feelings.

We've already touched on some of the benefits of noticing and controlling the breath, and further techniques are to follow; but here are some ideas to begin to familiarise children with the process.

- Pacing the breath. Tell the children to breathe out as fully as they can then to inhale-hold-exhale to a given count. They can decide for themselves what the pattern is to be – 2-4-2, 3-6-3 or whatever. The aim is to raise their awareness of the fact that slowing breathing brings a calming effect. A variation of this exercise is to use a metronome to set the pace, though again allowing each child to decide on the number of beats per breath that feels most comfortable.

  Breathing more fully in this way should never be forced. Also, keep to a relatively small number of full patterned breaths: if any child feels light-headed (through hyperventilating), tell him to breathe normally into a paper bag.

  Ideally as the in-breath begins the stomach should be pushed out, then contracted as the chest expands, with the process reversed for the out-breath. If children find this difficult however the refinement is not essential.

- Alternate nostril breathing. To do this, each child must place one index finger along the bridge of the nose with the thumb and middle finger positioned such that each nostril can be pressed closed separately. Once children have established a comfortable pattern of breathing by doing the previous exercise, get them to carry it out again, but now to close off each nostril alternately; so 2-4-2 for one nostril, then 2-4-2 for the other nostril. Again, four or five repetitions should be enough for most if not all children to feel the calming effects. This exercise also helps to develop concentration, given that the children are counting the breaths as well as remembering which nostril to close.

- Purposeful breathing. This is where taking one or two deep slow breaths is done for some other designated purpose. So you might suggest a 'stand back and think again' breath if a child tends to speak or act impulsively. Try a 'letting go of anger' breath. You or the children can think of other examples. The 'cleansing breath' is powerful. Here you suggest that good thoughts and feelings swish through the body as the child inhales, while bad thoughts and feelings are cleansed away on the out-breath. Four or five deep slow breaths keeping this in mind can work very effectively.

NOTICING YOUR OWN THOUGHTS

The mind is always active. Although we might find ourselves paying close attention to thoughts that stream through the conscious part of the mind (sometimes called 'cognitive space'), other thoughts swirl around the periphery of our conscious awareness, while subconscious mental processing goes on 24/7 all through our lives. Teaching children to become more aware of their thoughts allows them to have greater control over them, an ability known as metacognition. This in turn gives children more influence over their own feelings such that they can enhance positive feelings and 'turn down' or become more detached from unhelpful ones.

The key skill is not to become drawn into trains of thought so that we forget to pay attention to them. Getting lost in thought is fine if we are being entranced by a good story or listening to a fine piece of music, for example. Here we give tacit permission for the author or musicians to enter into the world of our mental story. But when it happens unintentionally we find ourselves idly daydreaming our time away or, worse, reliving unpleasant past experiences with all the attendant bad feelings such memories bring.

Here are some ideas to help children become more aware of their own thoughts.

- Read a piece of descriptive writing or an extract from a story. Then ask the children to note down what they noticed as they imagined the scene. Tell them that you are going to read the same piece again and that this time they will notice even more – colours, sounds, textures, etc. Again, ask them to jot down what they discover.
- Creative dialogue. You can demonstrate this with a volunteer, then get the children to work in pairs and try it for themselves. Say to your volunteer partner, 'Imagine someone walking down the High Street – tell me when you've done that.' When he says he has, ask him to tell you two interesting things about that person. When your partner has done this, suggest that this character meets a friend. Ask the child to tell you two interesting things about the friend. Continue to ask about details of clothing, facial features, voice, etc.

Keep the visualisation going for a few minutes, guiding in such a way that the dialogue between you and your partner is quiet and paced in a leisurely way. Your aim is to get your partner deliberately to focus his (or her) attention and to notice increasingly fine details in his imagination – the opposite of 'letting his imagination run away with him'.

A great longer-term benefit of children practising creative conversations in this way is that their imagined worlds will be much richer, whether they are visualising prior to writing, or while reading and listening to a story.

- The wise observer. This is a very old technique where you ask children just to 'stand back' from their thoughts as these go by, almost as if there was some other part of themselves watching their minds at work. Suggest that this 'other part' is wise and kind and a source of good advice. Children then create or remember experiences, making mental observations as they do this, such as 'I notice that memory is making me feel happy all over again' or 'I can remember being angry when that happened. Yes, I notice a bit of anger coming back now – but I can choose to remember something else right now.'

This kind of work helps children to gain greater access to positive thoughts and feelings while developing the capacity to modify the feelings attached to negative experiences.

MORE THINKING GAMES

More elaborate visualisations than the ones mentioned in 'Noticing your own thoughts' (p. 31) further develop children's metacognitive abilities and give them increasing control over what and how they think. Honing this skill is a valuable and necessary precursor to the activities you can offer them in the subsequent chapters of this book.

- Show the class a picture for 30 seconds or so, then, having removed it, ask them to imagine the image in as much detail as they can.
- Show time-lapse video clips, for instance of the way a tree changes through the year, or movies taken at super speed, such as a bullet passing through an apple or drops of milk hitting a hard surface. These are readily available online. Ask the children to recreate what they see in their mind's eye.
- Mentally eat an apple. Ask the children to imagine, for instance, an apple on the table in front of them. Instruct them to look at it carefully, noticing size, colours, any blemishes on the skin, etc. Then have them pretend to pick up the fruit, hold it in the hand, turn it this way and that, feeling the weight and texture of it. Get them to sniff the apple and attempt to conjure up its subtle and distinctive aroma. Then ask the children to eat the apple, again visualising as vividly as they can. They should take their time, experiencing the texture and taste of the fruit as they devour it.

Tip: 'Modelling the behaviour' by joining in yourself helps to stop some children feeling self-conscious in trying out this activity. Extend the work by asking the children themselves to come up with further examples.

- Thoughts on a pebble. One way of developing the skill of meditation is to use a physical object as the focus for attention and, later, for reflection and contemplation (more on this in Chapter 4).

Introduce the idea by using a pebble – either one stone that the whole class can concentrate on, or invite the children to bring in their own. Either way, the object will acquire greater significance the more it is used.

First, ask the class to focus their attention on the pebble (or whatever appropriate object individual children are using). You can combine this with children counting breaths or noticing their thoughts as they stream by. Ideally children do this without getting drawn in to 'chains of thought' that distract them from the primary task of keeping attention fixed on the stone. Regularly practise such quiet-sitting with the pebble as a focus. Begin with short periods of concentration and gradually lengthen these over time.

Tip: Some children may complain of being bored just sitting and staring at one object. Explain that being able to concentrate is a valuable skill in itself and that it paves the way for developing other beneficial mental and emotional skills. If any child has a special need with regard to attention, use your own judgement to modify the activity accordingly.

Repeating the task of concentrating on the pebble establishes a connection in the children's minds between the behaviour you want them to express (quiet sitting, concentration, feeling calm) and the pebble itself. In the field of personal development known as Neuro Linguistic Programming – NLP – this phenomenon is called an anchor. The aim is to anchor the behaviour of feeling calm / being aware of one's thoughts / concentration, with something that you and the children have under your conscious control.

At some point, ask the children to *imagine* the anchor rather than having it physically present. Explain that just thinking about the pebble (or whatever children are using) will have the same pleasing effect as if it was actually there.

- The pebble in the pond. Objects of concentration can also be used as metaphors. Ask the children to imagine the pebble being dropped into a still pool and notice the ripples spreading outwards over the water.

  Extend the activity by suggesting that this can represent our actions having consequences. Even our thoughts and feelings can affect other people, whether we intend them to or not. Also, it can be difficult to predict how far the 'ripples' of our actions might spread. Good thoughts, feelings and actions have beneficial effects, while vindictive thoughts, negative feelings and actions are usually detrimental.

  Note: Water is an ancient and powerful metaphor. You might want to spend time exploring this with the class using these ideas.

  – Each of us is like a drop in the ocean of existence.
  – The river of time.
  – The water cycle representing the cyclical nature of life: how we come from the earth and return to the earth.
  – Stormy weather / choppy seas representing difficult times in our lives (while 'plain sailing' stands for an easy passage).
  – A raindrop acting as a prism splitting white light into its constituent colours.
  – Thoughts like leaves drifting along on the stream.

  This last example might prove useful in showing children how to master the skill of letting their thoughts come and go. The wise observer part of the mind can sit on the riverbank and watch the leaves (which are our thoughts) sweep by.

- What if. This activity helps children to imagine consequences, to predict, to plan and create strategies for resolving problems. At the same time it encourages them to make creative connections and to look at issues in different ways. Remind them of the pebble-in-the-pool visualisation before you begin.

Suggest a what-if scenario to the class. It doesn't need to be realistic: the kinds of thinking that the children engage in to find practical solutions and/or reflect on consequences are the same as if they were tackling real-life situations.

So for example – what if all humans in the world suddenly shrank to six inches tall?

Append the main question with these subsidiary questions:

- What would the world be like?
- What problems would there be?
- How could we solve those problems?

As children become more confident in putting forward their ideas and more versatile in their thinking, consider giving them more taxing what-if challenges, including those they come up with themselves. Ultimately what-if thinking can be focused into areas of wellbeing such as emotional resourcefulness, forgiveness and living compassionately.

LOOKING AT SYMBOLS

The word 'symbol' derives from the Greek *symbolon*, a conjoining of *syn* meaning 'together' and *bole* meaning 'a throwing or casting of a projectile'. The meaning of the word evolved to take on the sense of 'a token used in comparisons to determine if something is genuine'. The idea that a symbol is a kind of metaphor representing something else that is *more than* the original object or idea was first recorded in 1590 in Edmund Spenser's epic poem 'Faerie Queene'.

Symbols can relate to an individual and have significance for that person only. Items of great sentimental value for instance can represent a wealth of memories and a lifelong relationship. Cultural symbols become powerful over time and take on a huge importance for millions of people. But whether relating to individuals, groups, nations or all of humankind, symbols 'point beyond themselves' insofar as they imply deeper and greater levels of meaning against which people can set and reflect on their values, beliefs, attitudes and decisions. It is in this context that studying the notion of symbolism generally and of particular symbols is beneficial within wellbeing education.

In the section called 'More thinking games' (p. 33) we looked at the idea of creating an anchor linking a given desired behaviour with an object (or a visualisation of that object) that is under a person's conscious control. The pebble used as our example serves as a 'positive visual anchor'; over time, as children see or imagine the pebble, they 'switch on' the behaviour of feeling calm, being aware of themselves in the present moment, concentrating their attention to a fine point and so on. In that sense a symbol of whatever kind can become a much more profound and powerful anchor that might affect a person's whole life. (For example, Steve remembers the astonishing image of the Earth rising over the Moon, taken by the crew of Apollo 8 in December 1968 and how that came to symbolise for him – and for millions of others no doubt – the fragility of the Earth, the 'outward urge' in the human heart to explore, investigate and understand; and the amazing achievements of modern technology. It also, still, causes him to reflect on the place of human beings in the universe.)

With that in mind, the symbols you choose to study need not be religious. Secular and 'culturally neutral' images are just as useful and beneficial.

Here are some ideas for looking at symbols.

- If children are unfamiliar with the concept of symbolism, show them some road signs and ask them to work out why a particular design, shape or colour stands for something else.

  Note: A sign is usually a brief message designed to be easily recognised and which does not affect us in any significant way. Unlike a symbol, a sign is brief, practical and to the point; it does not lend itself to deeper contemplation. A symbol, like poetry – to quote T. S. Eliot – can sometimes communicate before it is understood. Further, symbols can represent thoughts and feelings that we might find difficult to put into words.

You can extend this work by looking at familiar company logos, symbols in maths and the sciences. Turn the activity around… What could be the symbol for Geography, History, Biology, etc.?

- Human behaviour is amazingly complex. As a species we use a range of facial expressions and body language to represent how we think and feel. Help the class to compile of list of some of these.
- Plants, animals and features of the landscape have come to take on a symbolic quality in our imagination. At a less profound level of metaphor they are used as the basis for proverbs and folk sayings; for example, 'Every cloud has a silver lining.' However, the same things can point towards ideas of much greater significance. The ancient Chinese saying 'For the moon there is the cloud' touches upon the basic concept of the polarity and interdependency of all things and how this generates the essential creative dynamic of the universe. This is represented in a general way by the ancient Chinese symbol of Yin Yang (see Figure 1.5). Its design, simple but striking, reminds us that what appear to be opposite and contrary forces are actually complementary. This idea in turn throws up a wealth of philosophical speculations that you might explore with your class – without evil, how do we know what goodness is? If there was no ugliness, could we ever appreciate beauty? If there were sunshine but never any rain, what would happen to the world?

Test the children's inventiveness by showing them the Yin Yang symbol and asking questions such as these.

- If this image told us something about our feelings, what would we learn?
- What does this picture say about the way our society works?
- How does this picture help us to learn about the natural world?

Figure 1.5 Yin Yang

1   2

3   4

Figure 1.6 Abstract images

- Abstract images are full of potential for generating meaning. Show the class the pictures in Figure 1.6. Ask the children to imagine a fictional character and ask these questions.

  - What does image 1 say about our character's good qualities?
  - What does image 2 say about the character's bad side?
  - What does image 3 say about our character's past?
  - What does image 4 say about the character's ambitions?

Link objects to important life concepts. Ask children to bring a selection of ordinary objects or pictures of things into class. The task is to pick one object and decide how it can symbolise an idea from this list – truth, identity, belief, loyalty, thought, morality, reality, freedom, justice, power, death, happiness.

Looking at symbols is an effective way of learning about other times and cultures. There are numerous articles online and many books written on the subject. We've found that a very accessible book for classroom use is *The Illustrated Book of Signs & Symbols* by Miranda Bruce-Mitford (1996; see Bibliography).

CHAPTER 2

Jumpstart emotional resourcefulness

> We look before and after, and pine for what is not.
>
> ('To a Skylark', Percy Bysshe Shelley)

This chapter focuses on the link between thoughts and feelings and the idea that we can all potentially control our thinking to a greater degree, and therefore the way we feel about things, so building on the preparatory work we did in Chapter 1.

Synonyms for 'resourceful' include 'ingenious', 'imaginative', 'inventive' and 'creative'. The term 'resourcefulness' therefore implies that thoughts and feelings are themselves versatile resources, as well as defining the ability to devise elegant and effective ways of dealing with difficulties. It has been said that to solve a problem we often have to change our circumstances or change ourselves. Sometimes we have no control over our circumstances, but potentially we have far greater control over how we think and thus how we react to life's circumstances.

The notion of emotional resourcefulness is not new. As far back as the late nineteenth century the French psychologist Émile Coué was developing a method of self-improvement based on positive affirmations, most famously 'Every day in every way I am getting better and better'. Coué's belief was that by repeating the statement with an attitude of sincerity and firm expectation it became a self-suggestion that gradually influenced unhelpful ways of thinking. Subsequent major figures in the area of self-development include Dale Carnegie, known for books including *How to Stop Worrying and Start Living* (1972) and *How to Win Friends and Influence People* (1971), and Napoleon Hill and W. Clement Stone whose *Success*

Through a Positive Mental Attitude (1984) is also still widely read. (Steve still has his copy *of How to Stop Worrying and Start Living*. He bought it in 1972 during a stressful period and found its practical down-to-earth wisdom helped him enormously. Since then, just *holding* the book causes a positive shift of feelings – it has become a positive anchor; see the section 'More thinking games' in Chapter 1, p. 33.)

In the mid-noughties the psychologist and science writer Daniel Goleman revolutionised the field of self-improvement with his book *Emotional Intelligence* (2004) (subtitled 'and why it can matter more than I.Q.'), which gave scientific credence to many of the ideas and beliefs of earlier writers. The literature on the subject is now vast, such there can be no doubt that how we think and what we think has profound effects on our outlook on life.

TOP TIPS TO DEAL WITH WORRYING

Worrying has been compared to riding on a rocking horse – you put lots of effort into it but it gets you nowhere. The origin of the word lies in the Old English *wyrgan*, 'strangle'. Later it was used figuratively to mean 'harass', from which we get the modern sense of 'causing anxiety' (although the original definition surely also applies insofar as chronic worrying strangles our enjoyment of life).

There are many ways of dealing with the worry habit, many of them easily achievable. Here are some that have worked for us.

- Direct positive action. Worrying thrives on inaction. Doing something about it, however small an intervention, is almost always better than doing nothing.
- Talk it through. Keeping worry bottled up can be harmful and tends not to lead to a resolution of the issue. If it's not possible to talk to someone about the cause of the worry, writing about it often helps. Expressing the cause of the worry can clarify thoughts and may lead to a plan of action for dealing with the matter.
- Investigate a support network. This is an extension of the talk-it-through technique. Worrying can make us feel alone and isolated

when, in fact, there are probably many avenues we could explore to help us through our difficulties, real or perceived. Considering individuals, groups or organisations that might be able to help puts the 'direct positive action' principle to work very effectively.

- Be realistic. Worries are sometimes magnified in the mind such that they appear to be more serious than they actually are. Assessing the situation realistically often generates a healthy perspective on the issue. A robust four-step strategy is to: 1) write down precisely what you are worrying about; 2) write down what you can do about it, listing all the possibilities that come to mind; 3) decide exactly what you *will* do about it; and 4) immediately start to carry out your plan.
- Use your ability to recall the past and envision the future. Sometimes we worry about things that have already happened; the memories haunt us in the present moment. Using techniques like meditation allows us to put aside negative and unhelpful memories. Deciding that what's done is done – given that it can't now be undone – robs such thoughts of much of their harmful influence. Similarly it's all too easy to worry about what might lie in the future. These situations may or may not come about. If it's clear that a worrisome situation will arise we can ask, 'What's the worst that can happen?' and then plan to deal with that contingency should it occur. However, it's worth noting that Winston Churchill said that he'd had many problems in his life, most of which never happened. A very effective technique to use in conjunction with the above is to ask yourself if what seems so serious now will matter in five years' time.
- Gathering treasures. Take a little time to think of the good things you have in your life; people, places and things that have brought pleasure and happiness.
- Live in the present moment. We have touched elsewhere on the power of grounding ourselves in 'the now'. Practising techniques that help us to do this limits the influence that worrying thoughts can have. Dale Carnegie counselled something similar when he urged people to live in 'daytight compartments', while a much earlier source of wisdom advised that 'sufficient unto the day is the evil thereof'.
- Life overview. This draws on elements of several of the above. We can first recognise that whatever has happened, we have survived.

We are here now. Then in our imagination we can look ahead and envision positive possibilities that we desire to work towards. Thirdly we can realise ('make real' in our minds) that although worries can sometimes seem overwhelming at the moment, in the context of our whole lives and beyond that in the grand scheme of things, they are probably not so earth-shattering after all.

- Co-operate with the inevitable. If a situation can't be changed, no amount of worrying will alter that. Deciding to co-operate with the inevitable, in the sense of accepting that whatever it is will happen, can stop the worry habit in its tracks.

KEEP A MOODS JOURNAL

We've already mentioned that writing down whatever it is that's causing worry can help to alleviate it. Extend the idea by suggesting to children that they keep a moods journal. Here they write down how they feel, whether good or bad, either on an ad hoc basis as they need to and/or during a quiet time that you deliberately set aside for the purpose. The journal can be used in a number of ways.

- Write about good moods and positive feelings at the front of the book and negative or unpleasant feelings at the back. Use a simple icon such as a smiley face as a positive anchor when you read through the 'good feelings pages': draw the face on each page or use smiley stickers. Later, just imagining the smiley face will bring those good feelings back. Deliberately avoid re-reading the 'bad feelings pages' for a week or so. When you do go back to them you might find it hard to remember what caused the bad feelings, or realise that whatever did is no big deal after all.
- A variation on that last idea is to write down on a piece of paper what's worrying you or what has caused unpleasant feelings. Seal the note in an envelope and leave it for a week or so before opening. Again you might find that the problem never came to pass or that the cause of the bad feelings really wasn't that important after all.
- 'What would Superman do?' Pick a person you admire. This might be a fictional character or someone real. If that person had your problem, what would he or she do about it? Use your

imagination to come up with realistic solutions that you could achieve yourself.

- Vocabulary of feelings. Use a dictionary and thesaurus to find more names for emotions. Make a point of using your growing vocabulary when you write about how you feel. Think about what are the most appropriate words for the feelings you're having. Doing this means we can avoid extreme terms like 'hate' or 'loathe'.

Take it further

Create sets of 'feelings cards' based on the children's thesaurus activity. Split the class into groups and ask them to try the following.

- Pick a selection of cards and draw faces showing those emotions.
- Separate out good feelings and bad feelings. Sequence these according to how often the average person would be likely to experience them.
- Pick a small selection of cards and research the origins of the names of those feelings. So for instance anger comes from the Old Norse *angr*, meaning 'grief', and *angra*, meaning 'vex'. The word 'vex' in turn comes from the Latin *vexare*, to 'agitate or trouble'. Investigating word origins boosts the vocabulary and creates the opportunity to reflect on and look at feelings in a different way (so maybe, on reflection, I feel agitated about someone or something, rather than angry, which refers to a different feeling as far as I'm concerned).
- Put one of the cards in the middle of a large sheet of paper and create an association web, using words and pictures, to explore that feeling further. (Make it clear to the children that they do not need to write down any personal information and are certainly not required to remember any personal experiences relating to negative emotions.)

LOOK AT THINGS ANOTHER WAY

Being able to look at ideas, situations and experiences in different ways is one of the key elements of creative thinking (along with making new connections). The ability is no less important in the area of emotional resourcefulness and wellbeing. In fact, developing a greater sense of wellbeing and fulfilment *demands* the use of creative thinking to visualise, to reflect on different options and alternative possibilities, and to consider and reinterpret as a strategy for modifying unhelpful emotions.

Here are some activities you can try with your class.

- Expressions grid (Figure 2.1)

  - Pick one of the faces on the grid and ask children to describe its features – for example, eyes opened wide, mouth open, eyebrows raised. Are those same details shared by any other faces on the grid? What are those emotions called? Are they similar in any ways?
  - Pick one of the faces on the grid. Ask the children first to name the emotion on the circle-face, then to think of as many situations as possible that could cause that emotion. Encourage children to come up with positive and negative situations for the same circle-face if they can.

Figure 2.1 Expressions

- Use dice rolls to choose two or three circle-faces at random ('along the corridor and up the stairs'). Can the children come up with at least one situation that would cause both or all three of those emotions?
- Pick a circle face (using dice rolls if you wish) and ask children to describe what it feels like to experience that emotion. Encourage the use of similes and metaphors. Point out to the class that it isn't necessary for anyone to remember or talk about their own personal experiences. The aim of the activity is to define feelings more clearly in terms of body posture and other aspects of physiology such as heart rate, breathing rate, tensing or relaxing, etc.

- Situations

    Show the class the image in Figure 2.2. Ask the children what they think character A is doing to character B and why.

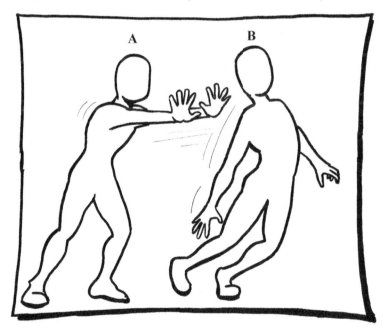

Figure 2.2 Generic push

Then show the class Figure 2.3 to demonstrate that it's easy to make assumptions or jump to a conclusion. Take the activity further by asking groups to use pairs of circle-faces from the grid; transpose them on to the heads of characters A and B, then think of a situation that would result in those emotions being expressed.

Show the class Figure 2.4. Ask the children to come up with a scenario to explain the burly man and the box that would cause the reactions shown by the four people surrounding. Ask the

A   B   C

Figure 2.3 Push scenarios

Figure 2.4 Situations and reactions

children to name the emotion each of these four people is displaying and to suggest a line of dialogue for each that could fit into the speech bubbles. Characters can be talking to each other or to themselves.

- Reactions

  Make copies of Figure 2.5 (the Reactions Template) and of Figure 2.1 (the circle-faces grid), resizing these as necessary. Split the class into groups. Ask the children to cut out the circle-faces. The task for each group now is to think of a situation, draw it in the centre of the template and then select circle-faces that reflect the feelings of the four characters witnessing it.

Literacy link: Show the class words that can mean different things depending on their context, such as 'good' or 'set'. Ask children to come up with sentences that reflect some of the different meanings.

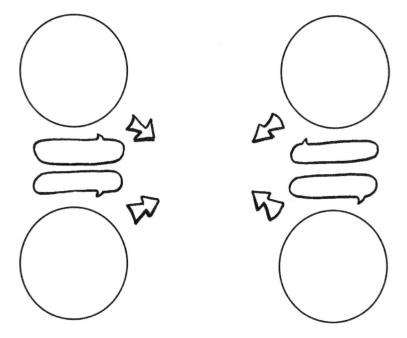

Figure 2.5 Reactions template

49

- Scenarios. Working individually, on a 12½ x 7½-centimetre file card, write a short scene about a situation likely to cause a particular emotion. Write the name of the emotion on the other side of the card. Swap with a class mate: does he or she link the same emotion to the situation you've written about? Working in a larger group, discuss whether you all feel the same way about a chosen situation. For instance, finding a £10 note in the street might make one person in the group feel excited, another feel concerned about the person who had lost it and maybe another feel guilty for spending money that hadn't been earned.
- Pick two cards naming similar emotions. Discuss the differences between them in terms of how they are experienced. So, for instance, does annoyance feel exactly the same as irritation? How does frustration differ from exasperation? Is amusement a 'bigger' emotion than enjoyment?

GENERALISING

This is the process of forming opinions, beliefs and attitudes that rest on incomplete knowledge and limited experience. A generalised view is often vague and yet can carry a strong emotional component, revealed in part by extreme language (see the note on 'obserpinions' in the section 'Observations of nature without judgement' in Chapter 1, p. 8).

The tendency to generalise is one of a number of ways of thinking that have been called 'cognitive distortions', insofar as they skew our view of the world in ways that are usually negative and unhelpful. Generalising goes hand in hand with the cognitive distortion of filtering, which is where, mostly subconsciously, we filter out certain aspects of our experience while selecting others that confirm the belief that the generalisation is correct. The danger of generalising is exactly that it can lead to a prejudiced view linked to a strong emotional response: the two things, viewpoint and emotion, are entangled, self-confirming and increasingly lead us away from the kind of independent, flexible and reflective thinking we advocate in this book. Racism, sexism, ageism and many other 'isms' are the unfortunate consequence of generalised thinking.

In terms of helping children to counter the bad habit of forming generalised opinions you might try the activities below. See also the sections 'Demand proof' (p. 57) and 'Mind your language' (p. 59) later in this chapter.

- Get the children to interlock their fingers. Use this as a visual analogue for the way of thinking that we call generalising. One hand represents the vague overarching viewpoint itself and the other hand represents the emotional response that goes with it. Now ask the children to clench their hands together even tighter. This is how generalisations grow, where the viewpoint and the feelings become more and more tightly locked. Ask the children to notice that squeezing fingers together like this becomes uncomfortable or even painful – it hurts. Make the point that generalising turns us into robots; we're not thinking clearly. The more extreme the generalisation, the more it can hurt other people too.

  Finally, ask the children to unclasp their hands and notice how pleasant this feels, just to separate out the thinking from the feeling. Let the hands rest relaxed palms up in the lap for a few moments.

- Choose a topic such as 'food' and present the class with a number of statements that relate to it. Make some of them purely factual such as 'milk contains vitamins including B1, B2, B3 and B5'. Make others a little more controversial such as 'processed food is bad for you' or 'people who eat the wrong foods or too much food become fat'. You'll notice that these statements are already edging towards being generalisations. Offer some statements that are even more contentious such as 'if you become obese it's your own fault'...

  Important note: You will of course need to use your own discretion as to which statements you choose, bearing in mind that some children in the class might already be very sensitive to the issue you are exploring.

Now ask the children to separate the statements into two categories, facts and opinions, then write the opinions on scraps of paper. Draw a line on a larger sheet of paper and arrange the scraps along it in terms of how extreme they are. Note that this is to be done irrespective of whether or to what extent any child agrees or disagrees with any statement.

- Take a controversial statement (ideally one that doesn't apply to any child in the class). Ask the children to decide how far they agree or disagree with it; use a 1–6 scale where 1 is 'strongly agree' and 6 is 'strongly disagree'.

Now remind the class of the Big Six open questions – who, what, where, when, why and how. Split the class into smaller groups. Get each group to write the statement on a large sheet of paper and around it any open questions they can think of to test its veracity. Suggest that some of the questions could form the basis of a piece of research that hopefully will highlight the generalisation for the limited piece of thinking it is.

- 'Sombunall'. The maverick writer-philosopher Robert Anton Wilson coined this term to mean 'some but not all'. It is a powerful mechanism for restoring balance in the presence of unreflective generalisations. So when we hear the opinion 'teenagers are lazy' we can immediately modify our response by saying 'sombunall teenagers are lazy'. This necessarily implies that some are not lazy. We can go further and suggest that 'sombunall teenagers are lazy sombunall of the time', followed by the application of the Big Six open questions.

A further refinement is to use words such as 'appear' or 'seem'. 'Sombunall teenagers seem to be lazy'; this prompts further investigation into whether we are talking about laziness in all cases every time, or whether there are other possible explanations.

ON BALANCE

Another common cognitive distortion (see 'Generalising') is 'polarised' or all-or-nothing / either-or thinking, where some people swing to one extreme or the other: there's no middle ground. So if I fail to get excellent marks in Maths I think, 'I'm useless at Maths.' Words to look out for in thinking like this include 'never', 'always', 'totally', 'completely', 'utterly', 'useless', 'hopeless' and so on.

As with other kinds of skewed thinking, a first useful step is to notice when it's happening and then apply one or more techniques to redress the balance and gain a more realistic perspective. Here are some ideas.

- Say it like it is. So using the example above, instead of saying, 'I'm useless at Maths', recognise what actually occurred – so maybe, 'I scored 53 per cent in my last Maths test'.

  Apropos this point, during a writing workshop Steve noticed that one boy had written 'seperate' instead of 'separate'. When the teacher pointed out the misspelling the boy – without any sarcasm – replied, 'Yes but I got the other seven letters right.' (To the teacher: how do you think you would react to the boy's comment? Would you be annoyed at his backchat or arrogance? Amused at his witty reply? Or would you respond in another way?)

- Still learning. We never stop learning (this being a generalisation we approve of!). While we need not condone laziness or lack of effort, we can recognise the fact that a less-than-perfect score is often a reflection that children are still learning about the world, still trying to master complex ideas and processes.
- The continuum of life. If we draw a line to represent the full spectrum of human ability, or whatever other aspect of our lives we choose to think about, then it's almost inevitable that we will have to position ourselves somewhere along the line and not at either end. Steve likes writing stories. There will always be more popular / successful / profound authors than him and ones that are less so. That's just how it is. And that need have nothing to do with Steve's efforts to become the best writer he can be.

However much he improves, there will still always be writers who are better. This puts us in mind of the wise adage that practice doesn't make perfect; it makes better.

• On balance. Help the children to establish this useful thinking skill. Whenever they catch themselves thinking a negative thought, balance it out by deliberately searching for an equivalent positive one. So 'I was really mean to my sister this morning' can be balanced with the memory of being kind to her at the weekend. Thinking this way counters the tendency to drip-feed ourselves with negative impressions.

STORIES WE TELL OURSELVES

The same resources of memory and imagination that can be so empowering for us may also lead to anxiety, worry and fear. It's all too easy to make false assumptions, speculate in the absence of the facts and jump to negative conclusions – in effect to create imagined narratives that stir up further negative thoughts and unpleasant feelings, but which have little to do with the reality of the situation.

Help children to dampen the tendency to 'spin unhelpful yarns' by trying these techniques.

• 'Yes but maybe…' Give the children a situation to think about, such as 'My friend hasn't replied to my text message'. Ask the class to come up with as many reasons as possible why this might be so. Someone with a negative outlook could easily jump to the conclusion that the lack of a reply was because that person no longer wanted to be friends, but there could be many other explanations.

Encourage the children to be as creative in their ideas as possible. Accept even the most outrageous possibilities such as, 'Yes but maybe my friend was abducted by aliens / swallowed his mobile phone by mistake / fell through a time portal into the past.' This is not being frivolous: once the ideas are in, rank them on a scale of likelihood from 1 to 10. Take the negative conclusion 'he no longer wants to be friends' and decide where on the scale it would fit *after examining any other evidence to support that conclusion.* So the no-longer-friends scenario could be labelled likely only if other strong pieces of evidence were found.

Encourage the children to apply this technique whenever they spin their own yarns that cause them to worry.

- Centre yourself. Yarn-spinning draws us deeper into the imagined scene such that we disconnect more from the present moment. Put a stop to that by using these techniques.

  - Breathing slowly and deeply for a few moments.
  - Bringing yourself back to the here-and-now by noticing what's around you.
  - Stepping back from the thoughts and feelings that are causing you to be anxious.
  - Giving yourself some positive messages by thinking of pleasant experiences.

SNAP JUDGEMENTS

- The mind works quickly. Demonstrate this to the children by making a list of objects, some ordinary and mundane – football, pencil, cat; others more exotic – palm tree on a beach, a purple aeroplane, a flying pig. Read the list to the class with a pause of a few seconds between each item. Ask the children to imagine each one as vividly as they can. Most children can create a mental image of these objects in a flash.
- Follow up the activity by pointing out that the mind can make snap judgements just as quickly, but that these are only potentially harmful if they are not examined, questioned and reflected upon. Create another list to test the claim, this time making the items possibly more controversial, insofar as they 'tempt' the mind to judge – immigrants, overweight people, people with ginger hair, queue jumpers, the police... Snap judgements can be positive as well as negative of course, but the point is that they are made virtually instantly and as it were 'allowed to go by' unquestioned. If this happens often enough

then it heightens the tendency for us to pre-judge; to have formed a viewpoint that predisposes us to accept further snap judgements even more uncritically.

As with many aspects of emotional resourcefulness the first necessary step is to *notice* the thoughts and feelings we have. These constitute the 'raw material' that we can then work on by applying other techniques.

Strategies for modifying the tendency to make snap judgements include the following.

- Wearing a rubber band around the wrist. When you notice the appearance of a snap judgement, snap the band as a reminder not to do it again. This simple technique can be remarkably effective in conditioning the mind to stop and think first before judging.
- Making a negative remark about yourself in response to you making a snap judgement about someone else. The act of self-criticism often evokes the response of 'Yes but that's not fair' or 'I'm only like that some of the time'. These qualifications can then be applied to the person you've judged.
- Creating an association web around the focus of the person or type of person you've judged. Allow linked ideas to flow without effort, but notice how as the web grows you can come to deeper insights about why the judgement was there in the first place.
- Imagining a pyramid, which represents the person you are judging. Reflect on the fact that what you see (and on which you might have based your judgement) is just the tip of the pyramid. Beneath and beyond this lies that person's much greater personality and their whole life experience. What we see of each other moment by moment is just a tiny part of who we are.

TURN THAT FROWN UPSIDE DOWN

If you accept that thoughts, feelings and physiology are connected, then deliberately altering our facial expression and body posture can help to modify how we feel and what we think.

- Help the children to become more aware of this by showing pictures of different facial expressions reflecting a range of emotions. Ask the class to identify the feelings and to describe the facial expression in some detail.
- Extend the activity by showing the class different body postures – you don't need to do these yourselves; there are plenty of suitable images online. Again ask for descriptions of each posture and the emotion(s) it expresses.
- Ask the children to recall an experience that annoyed them or that made them a little upset (not very upset or frightened). As they have the recollection and notice the associated feelings rising, get them to smile and even laugh and notice what that does to the memory-and-feelings.
- Mention the concept of 'radiators and drains'. Some people radiate enthusiasm, friendliness, kindness and interest in the world. Others with a perpetually gloomy outlook drain you; they are exhausting to be with and draw you in to their same dismal world. Making an effort to 'turn that frown upside down' helps to limit the effect of people who are drains. Deliberately cultivating an attitude of interest and enthusiasm is a powerful way of becoming a radiator.

DEMAND PROOF

Many of the ways of thinking that lead to worry and anxiety flourish in the absence of evidence. Generalising, black-or-white thinking, fearing the worst, making assumptions and snap judgements continue to thrive if they are not questioned.

We have looked at several ways of countering these unhelpful tendencies; demanding proof (from ourselves as much as from others) adds a powerful tool to our repertoire of strategies for boosting our wellbeing.

Three powerful ways of 'demanding proof' are:

- checking beliefs against the hard evidence and facts (what we know)

- looking for any assumptions or judgements not based on fact (what we thought we knew)
- asking questions if possible or necessary to get closer to the true situation (what we need to ask to reach the truth).

Tip: This strategy is a variation of the three-step approach to handling information more generally. The steps are: 1) What do we know? 2) What do we think we know? and 3) What questions do we need to ask to be sure or at least clearer? Children who are encouraged to use the three-step method become far more active learners, though be prepared to spend more time helping them to answer their increasingly incisive questions. This puts us in mind of the ancient oriental aphorism: 'The grass is green and the sky is blue – great Chinese wisdom. The grass is not green and the sky is not blue – great Chinese wisdom.'

Below are a couple of other techniques that can be used with the demanding proof approach.

- Take as you find. Encourage children to base their opinions on actual experiences and situations and even then to make them provisional if all of the facts of the matter are not available. This is linked to the 'we'll see' way of looking at things. Earlier in the book we quoted Winston Churchill who said that he'd had many problems in his life, most of which had never happened. Creating future crises in the imagination helps no one, especially if that same power to imagine fails to come up with some possible solutions at the same time.
- 'I don't know.' It's fine to admit that we don't know something that can't be known. Steve was once told by an acquaintance that 'we're all shamed as children'. Perhaps that person had felt shamed in childhood and maybe she has known others who were too; but to believe that it happens to everyone is unrealistic. In our opinion to respond to her assertion with an I-don't-know seems a reasonable and emotionally healthier option.

MIND YOUR LANGUAGE

We saw earlier how 'extreme' language can feed generalisations and negative self-talk. Words like 'must', 'all', 'always', 'never', 'can't', etc., contribute to a rigid way of thinking and a blinkered outlook on the world. The problem can be more deeply rooted however and less easy to spot.

Our language is laced with metaphors. (Did you spot that one and, just now, 'deeply rooted'?) They tend to run in the background often unnoticed and yet have a powerful influence on the way we view the world. As such metaphors are much more than just a literary device: they are processes that actively shape our thinking and the way we feel.

As a precursor to introducing this concept to the children, consider the metaphors used in education. We have aims, targets and league tables; strategies are robust and the curriculum is rigorous; children can be pushed and stretched and, in groups, form cohorts. These metaphors come from the world of sport and the military – a cohort derives from the Latin and means 'a company of soldiers'.

By way of experiment, apply the language of gardening to the world of learning, where now we have cultivating, growing, flourishing, nurturing, blossoming, seedlings, shoots, fruits, harvests, tending, abundance, organic, natural, diversity, environment and hundreds more – type 'words related to gardening' into a search engine to verify this. Perhaps like us you find that spending some time thinking about education in this way alters your perception of what it is and how it can be conducted.

- Take a concept like 'learning' and say to the class, 'If learning was like gardening, what sentences can you think of to explore that idea?'

Vary the activity by asking for some creative linking…

- How is failure like a hero?
- How are feelings like a fairground?

- How is a fact like a butterfly?
- How is writing like a landscape?

Vary the game by saying 'The mind is like a butterfly because…?' Then ask the children to come up with more comparisons for the mind – insist on at least a dozen to demonstrate what an amazing and versatile thing their thinking is.

HAVING A PLAN

The ability to create a clear yet flexible plan helps to dispel frustration and the sense of 'stuckness' that often goes with it. Earlier we saw how 'direct positive action' – the idea that doing something is better than doing nothing – tackles worry head-on and goes a long way to promoting a sense of wellbeing.

Here are some useful questions that you can ask children, or that they can ask themselves, when they want a route map towards a more desirable state.

- What do you want to achieve?

  Make sure the child frames this positively, so not 'I don't want such poor grades' but 'I want better grades'. Note also that achievement comes from self-endeavour and brings its own earned satisfaction.

- Do you think you need to make any of those words clearer?

  So, for instance, what does the child mean by 'better'? How much better? Better in what way?

- What will it feel like to have achieved what you want?

  This 'positive future projection' links the vision of success with the pleasant feelings that go with it and primes the child to make the effort to move forward.

- What steps will you take to get there?

Encourage the child to be as precise as possible in formulating what needs to be done and in what order. Append the question, 'How will you know you've taken that step?' to each one.

If the child thinks that one or more things might hinder progress, try the 'cycle challenge' to overcome the difficulties.

- What's stopping you? (Followed by the child's response.)
- What could you do? (Ask the child to come up with at least one option and, if more than one, to choose the most effective.)
- What's stopping you?
- What could you do?

Cycle the child's thinking through these same questions until the issue is resolved.

Even the most carefully formed plan cannot guarantee success of course, but a clear and definite plan does increase its chances. Once the plan has been acted upon, offer the child the opportunity to reflect on it.

- How did things go?
- What worked best and why?
- What didn't work so well?
- What did you learn?
- What will you do differently next time?

We'll come back to this in the sections of reflective thinking and writing later in the book.

Reference: Bowkett and Percival's *Coaching Emotional Intelligence in the Classroom* (2011).

QUOTES

Inspirational quotes are potent when they convey meaning and significance with an emotional charge. We have found that children can have great insight into what inspiration means – 'when you are inspired you get lots of ideas', 'it makes you excited and want to do something', 'a great quote says in a few words what it would take you a long time to explain', 'inspiration makes you glow inside', 'sometimes reading one makes me feel lighter…'.

We believe that the best way to use inspirational quotes is to display them one at a time, prominently placed, and to spend some time talking with the class about what thoughts it evokes. We have seen classrooms where a rash of quotes has been stuck up on the walls, often photocopied on to A4 sheets, now yellowed and with edges curling. These quickly become invisible to the children, even if initially they were discussed.

Choosing quotes is a personal matter, of course; there's an endless supply online. Here are some that we like on the theme of wellbeing and creativity.

> Out of clutter, find simplicity. From discord, find harmony. In the middle of difficulty, find opportunity.
>
> (Albert Einstein)

> People almost always become what others think they are. Becoming is almost always the product of expectations.
>
> (Traditional saying)

> Understanding is caused by speech.
>
> (Thomas Hobbes)

> The person who can't make a mistake can't make anything.
>
> (Abraham Lincoln)

> Of all the liars in the world, sometimes the worst are our own feelings.
>
> (Rudyard Kipling)

> Someone who carries his own lantern has no need to fear the dark.
>
> (Anonymous)

CHAPTER 3

Jumpstart meditation and relaxation

Sometimes I sits and thinks and other times I just sits.
(Attributed to various sources)

WHAT IS MEDITATION?

The term 'meditation' has many different meanings with the word broadly translating from the verbs of 'thinking, pondering and contemplating'. This pastime has become particularly popular in the Western world over the last few decades with an openness towards the peaceful and satisfied images of the Tibetan monks as a stress-reducing solution for today's busy world. Various traditional references relate to 'getting to know your mind', the art and discipline of understanding yourself while focused on a particular thought or subject. For the purposes of the book we are looking at a non-religious approach to the benefits of meditation and relaxation for young people. The practice of meditation has numerous benefits and characteristics that aid learning or, to put it another way, using these techniques can make you a better learner. The Building Learning Power (BLP) work of Professor Guy Claxton outlines how to make children effective lifelong learners by equipping young learners with the skills to solve problems. Successful learners draw on their developed skill set when they are stuck and importantly this is the point when they are going to learn something new. Thinking through this 'being stuck' part of learning something new is where our range of skills and experiences help us through this confusion and come out the other side of being stuck with the answer, which equals learning something new. This point is significant when developing pupils' resilience to conquering problems when they become stuck during their learning (see Figure 3.1).

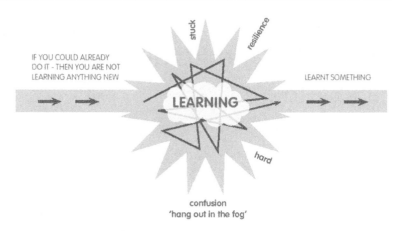

IF YOU COULD ALREADY
DO IT - THEN YOU ARE NOT
LEARNING ANYTHING NEW

LEARNING

LEARNT SOMETHING

stuck

resilience

hard

confusion
'hang out in the fog'

Figure 3.1 Learning graphic

As this illustration demonstrates, pupils need to draw on a range of skills that can help them solve the problem (and come out of the other side) which will result in having learnt something new. Meditation has a part to play in this model as one of the tools that sharpens those learning skills when we are learning something new. In addition, the wellbeing advantages of meditation and relaxation supplement its learning enhancements which make it a valuable addition to children's learning in the classroom and at home.

In our fast and changing world, utilising the benefits of meditation in our 'tool box of skills' that helps solve the unknown problems of tomorrow are significant features of today's successful learners.

THE BENEFITS OF MEDITATION

There are numerous benefits to meditation from a teacher and parent perspective which can develop and grow young learners' minds. These can be divided into three sections.

1. Social skills and wellbeing – the ability to deal and resolve stressful situations, increased tranquillity and the ability to deal with stress, dealing with playground conflicts, enhanced self-

understanding, enhanced spiritual development, help in finding 'inner peace', reduced tension/stress, headaches and blood pressure, less anxious, help with relationships, voice of self-criticism is quieter, easier to make decisions, get a feeling for who we are. A very useful tool in reducing stress during exams or SATS tests.

2. Enhanced sleep – enhancing physical relaxation and enabling more restful sleeps while providing greater energy. This area is tackled later on the chapter but in a nutshell the relaxation activities help children, parents and teachers to switch off at night time. This may be going to sleep or generally switching off during our leisure time.

3. Developing learning skills – improved concentration and memory, more control over the thought process, improved mindfulness, improved creative thinking skills, improved memory, helps philosophical enquiry, more productive learners. Awareness of the mind and 'inner self', the ability for quiet concentration, enables you to focus on a clearly defined stimulus, develops your reflection, attention and focus.

This is another tool in the Building Learning Power tool box as previously described on p. 63.

In summary, the benefits of meditation include improvements in:

- learning (and test scores!)
- concentration and memory
- visualisation skills
- creative and thinking skills
- tranquillity
- ability to deal with stress
- mindfulness
- self-understanding, developed emotional intelligence and social skills
- spiritual development.

More than that, meditation/relaxation is a peaceful activity that gives us greater energy, and helps us to live in the now and become more productive. Importantly it gives us a more restful sleep, reduces tension and anxiety, and even helps our relationships! It all seems too good to be true.

Thinkpoint: Your mind talks to you every few seconds, throwing out ideas. Spend a minute just noticing the different thoughts and share the random range of ideas that occur.

- The muddy jar

  Fill a jam jar with water and a tablespoon full of mud. Replace the lid. Explain to the pupils that the jam jar represents your mind. Shake the jar and watch as the mud swirls around and the water becomes cloudy. The mud represents your thoughts which can be busy, random and chaotic. Sometimes you need to calm your mind for greater clarity of thought or personal relaxation so you can rationalise your thoughts. Meditation and breathing helps slows things down. Watch as the mud (your thoughts) slows down and settles as the water becomes clearer. Discuss the benefits of achieving this within your mind, especially after a hectic playtime or before an important music performance, written test or before you go to sleep. (See Figure 3.2.)

- Your mind is amazing

  Outline to the pupils that some thoughts we know are made up, others we believe to be true and others we know to be true. Share some thoughts with the children and highlight the skill of filtering out the true from the fake thoughts.

  Filtering: Outline five possible thoughts. Ask the pupils to state if they are true (or possible) or false (nonsense).

  - The sky is blue (true).
  - Working hard makes you better at things (true).
  - My friend looked at me in a funny way which means they were saying nasty things about me (false).
  - Cheery smiling help solves arguments (true).
  - Everything I think is true (false).

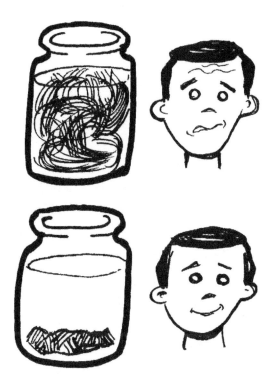

Figure 3.2 The muddy jar

- What can you do with your mind?

  Try the following 'mind exercises'.

  - Remember your last birthday.
  - Describe what you were wearing yesterday.
  - Recall your favourite meal.
  - Describe your route home from school to another person.
  - Think of five things that are really important to you.
  - Picture the face of someone in your family.

  Imagine the following things; birds singing, the rain, a creaky door, water going down a plug hole, wind in the trees, laughter, a baby crying, a plane flying by... Ask pupils to suggest further ideas for the class to think of.

- Remembering the past

This is how you can frame the activity for the children...

I'd like you to think back to a day when you were enjoying yourself. Maybe it was a birthday, or a time when you were on holiday.

Try to remember exactly how you felt when you woke in the morning, and what you did during the day.

Go through as many details as you can – the things you said, the things people said to you, the clothes you wore, the objects you touched, the things you saw. Go right through to bedtime, and remember how you felt when the day was over.

Follow up: Ask the children to recall what they were doing yesterday and then the same day the previous week.

- Kim's game (see Figure 3.3).

Each child or group has a pencil and paper. You will need a timer, a tray, and a range of everyday objects (at least 20) as different from each other as possible (e.g. pencil, ruler, spoon, apple, etc.).

Place the objects on a tray; the children look at the tray for a given amount of time.

Remove the tray; the children list as many objects as possible.

Repeat, but remove one object; the children guess the missing object.

- Memory of home

Ask the pupils to draw from memory the layout of their homes.

Figure 3.3 Kim's game

Take it further and draw a picture of the street where they live.

Ask pupils to draw in succession and from memory a number of everyday objects (lamp post, telephone, tree, bird, comb, teddy, bed, horse, fish, stairs, table, spoon, TV, etc.).

- Upside-down world

    Show the pupils a picture of a familiar scene. Turn the picture upside down; get the pupils to draw it. This activity develops visual and spatial experience.

Thinkpoint: 'Spending time with yourself' – help children to realise that just sitting and spending time with yourself is not 'doing nothing', nor is it boring if approached in the right way. This is a precursor to the idea of reflective breathing and meditation practice explored later in Chapter 4.

HELPFUL HINTS FOR MEDITATIONS AND RELAXATIONS

There is no set way to organise a class or home session but a focus on the self and a non-competitive approach are central. At this point it is important to outline the distinction between meditation and a relaxation as they are similar but different activities. For the purpose of this book meditations are short focused activities that generally last no longer than a few minutes where the children are either standing or sitting upright to complete the activity. Relaxation activities are longer sessions (up to 8 minutes for children) and usually involve lying down with a range of focuses compared to the singular attention focus of a meditation. During a relaxation you concentrate on and visualise different ideas or feelings while meditation is just concentrating on one single focus.

Here are some general hints for meditation and relaxation.

- Don't force the children to take part (although everyone joins in from our experience).

- Set the scene for calmness so the children approach the session in the right frame of mind.
- Let the parents know what you are doing to avoid misunderstandings.
- Initially use the word 'relaxation' rather than 'meditation'.
- To begin with keep the sessions short.
- Meditate every day, in the same place and the same time (start of the day, after playtimes and end of the day are good times).
- Keep it simple. Remove shoes.
- Explain to children this is a time for them; it's not a time to worry or talk to their friends.
- Children need to be sitting/laying while not directly looking at or touching other pupils.
- If children lie down they may fall asleep especially during relaxation activities, so keep these sessions short.
- Avoid relaxation activities immediately after lunch as some children will fall asleep!
- Start all sessions with a breathing activity.
- Use calm music to help meditation and relaxation.
- End sessions by sitting in a circle and breathing correctly for three breaths.
- Sit still for 20 seconds in silence.
- Consider setting up a relaxation/meditation room in a quiet area of school.

CREATE YOUR OWN RELAXATION ROOM, THE 'BLUE ROOM'

Although all the activities in this book can be successfully completed in a classroom or bedroom, nothing is as magical as creating your own room dedicated to meditation and relaxation. In 2002 at Latchmere School in Kingston, London, we created our own relaxation space where classes of children could practise a range of wellbeing skills including meditation, relaxation and peer massage. Dedicating a whole room to meditation in a busy school may be impractical but it is certainly worth it. Back in 2002 we managed to persuade the head teacher to renovate an eccentric attic room up a flight of twisty stairs in the school. It didn't cost much to convert the space. The room had blue walls, soft lighting and blue padded sofas that could seat a whole class. The room is now used by all the classes in a busy four-form primary school and has certainly withstood the test of time and was highly praised by Ofsted in 2009. Unsurprisingly the room quickly became known as the Blue Room and is still popular to this day. (See Figure 3.4.)

When we asked people at the school to describe their experience of the room, this is was they said:

> 'I see the benefits daily. I was struggling to get to sleep but from then on I have never struggled. Also I've learnt how to relax in different circumstances.'
>
> (Year 6)

> 'An oasis in a busy day. One Year 6 boy is now able to sit or lie perfectly still for half an hour. He normally found it difficult to sit still in class and talked constantly.'

Figure 3.4 Blue Room

'At the end I invariably feel good about myself.'

(Teaching Assistant)

'We all feel a lot calmer after each session and I've learnt how to breathe properly. Also I can see pictures clearly in my mind, these visualisations have helped my imagination and writing.'

(Year 5)

'At bedtime I used to feel stressed and hassled, always thinking of the negative nerve-racking things, not those that made me feel calm and proud of myself. Controlling your mind is a very powerful and useful skill.'

(Year 6)

'I don't get ill as much and I have more friends since I started meditation.'

(Year 4)

'It helps you get out of your own way.'

(Year 5)

Others spoke movingly of defusing playground conflicts, how it's great to have lessons in a special room, coping with arguments and difficult choices, handling friendships/emotions, family problems – and doing those tests!

BREATHING: THE STARTING POINT

Calming, noticing and controlling the breath is the starting point to any meditation or relaxation activity. Followers of yoga will recognise this importance while we all subconsciously take a deep breath when nervous or facing a big challenge. The key learning point is to take longer, slower breaths deep into the stomach so oxygen can be absorbed into the body, which naturally calms us down. The reverse is true of light quick breathing (shallow breathing) that hyperventilates the body bringing carbon dioxide into the body instead of oxygen.

Highlighting the importance of good breathing (deep breaths into the stomach) compared to lazy breathing (short or shallow breaths) is central to successful meditations and relaxations.

- Tips for good breathing

During meditation activities the body needs to be upright not slumped, head upright, both feet flat on the floor and hands resting on lap (see 'Royal breathing', p. 75). During relaxations children can sit or lay down; there is less emphasis on posture with relaxation breathing. Accentuate to the pupils that breathing is a natural thing to do; try to breathe quietly. Children have a tendency to blow the air out loudly and tense up as they start the breathing. The key is quiet and gentle while taking steady deep breaths. (See Figure 3.5.)

Figure 3.5 Sitting position

Breathing activities

- Royal breathing. To develop a good posture when breathing, encourage the child to sit upright and proud like the queen or king. Focus on a straight back and upright shoulders with head and knees facing forwards. Remind the child of this posture at the start of each session.
- Balloon breathing. Close the eyes and put one hand on the stomach. Imagine your stomach is a soft coloured balloon. Breathe in gently inflating the balloon; breathe out slowly to deflate the balloon. Breathe as above. Start to breathe normally; focus only on the out-breath.

Breathe in through your nose for 3 seconds (hold for 3 seconds); breathe out through your mouth slowly for 5 seconds. Repeat ten times.

As above, when you breathe out, focus on a warm glow in your stomach; focus on this feeling as you continue to breathe.

Fun breathing activities

- In and out through the nose (3 seconds each way).
- Counts with even numbers, e.g. 2 in 2 out, 4 in 4 out, 6 in 6 out, 8 in 8 out.
- Counts with uneven numbers, e.g. 2 in 4 out, 3 in 6 out, 4 in 8 out. Experienced meditators should be aiming for 8 in 24 out!
- Slow down exhalations using 'hissing teeth', as slow a release as possible, hissing to control the out-breath.
- Hold (air retention). Only do this for short periods of time with children, e.g. 4 in, hold for 4, breathe out for 4.
- Hahs! Breathe in for 4, hold for 4, with a 'HAH!' expel the air from the lungs

Become aware of your breathing. Focus upon the feeling of coolness at your nose when you breathe in, and the feeling of warmth as you breathe out.

- Nostril breathing. Close one of your nostrils with your finger; breathe in through your other nostril for 6 while breathing out through your mouth. Swap nostrils and repeat.

  Repeat alternating nostrils after each breath.

  Breathe normally, slowly counting to 10 in your head. Visualise the numbers using different colours for each. Repeat ten times. If you lose count, start back at one.

  Breathe deeply. While breathing in, cross over palms and fingers, lock and turn hands inside towards chest; as you breathe out undo this process. Repeat three times and then swap hands over and repeat.

- Taking out the rubbish. Breathe in through your nose for 3 seconds (hold for 3 seconds); breathe out through your mouth slowly for 5 seconds. Repeat.

  As you breathe in, feel the positive energy and strength entering your body. When you breathe out, say goodbye to the negative feelings and unwanted thoughts.

  Repeat using the colours of light (in-breath) and dark (out-breath).

- Removing the grey. This activity removes the negative energy from your body. We have chosen the colour grey for this activity. Standing up, gently breathe, imagine your body is full of the negative colour grey. Watch as the colour drains from your body through your feet into the ground being replaced by an energising white colour. This should take 50 seconds to remove the grey and replace with an uplifting colour or feeling.

MEDITATION ACTIVITIES

These activities work best after a few minutes of calm breathing.

- Rise and fall. Listen to the rise and fall of the breath; notice as your body drops and rises during this meditation. Inwardly say the words 'rise' and 'fall' as the breath changes.
- Noticing. Focus your attention on the breath; become aware of the moment when the in-breath turns to the out-breath. Try to pinpoint the exact moment when this happens. In your head say the word 'now' at this precise moment.
- Magic specs walk. Talk to the pupils about enjoying the beautiful world around us – highlight that sometimes we are in too much of a rush and miss the wonderful things around us. All we need to do is slow down.

Ask the pupils to put on their magic spectacles and look around the classroom/bedroom. What do they see? What have they missed? Take a walk, noticing as many things as possible. Share afterwards. (See Figure 3.6.)

- Being still. Stillness is a key skill for meditation and relaxation activities. Younger children will find this difficult at first so the sessions should be built up gradually. Keep them light and fun by using characters to help stillness, like pretending to be a snowman or statue. Pretend you're a sentry who is on guard, watching carefully everything that goes in and out of the city.

Figure 3.6 Magic specs

- Frozen. Sit totally still for 20 seconds, then 40 seconds, then 1 minute. Repeat while standing (legs slightly bent, arms to the sides, shoulders loose, feet apart and level with shoulders). Notice which parts of the body start to feel warm or ache during the activity; keep breathing steady.
- Mind palace. Close your eyes and scan your whole body. If you notice any discomfort in any part of your body, breathe some extra oxygen into that part. Once your body is completely relaxed, think about how wonderful your mind is, how it can remember so many things. With your eyes still closed, visualise the following things using your wonderful mind; your smile, you dancing or singing, a favourite pet, your best friend, your bedroom, any pleasant place.

Thinkpoint: Discuss how easy or difficult this challenge was. Highlight that the four main attributes of meditating at this early stage are breathing, posture, stillness and returning to the focus when the mind drifts.

- Sounds. Sit and listen to all the sounds in the room and outside the room. Fully focus on careful listening to every sound. Decide what type of sound it is, the frequency/pitch – pleasant sound/ unpleasant sound.
- Turn it down. Listen to the chatter in your mind for a few moments. Imagine your thumb is the volume switch to the voice in your head, slowly turn the thumb quietening the mind. Slowly turn the volume up and then gently down again.
- The Now. Being conscious of the present moment has many advantages in understanding and enjoying what you are doing right now. Living in the moment, i.e. appreciating what you are doing right now, involves thinking and *being* in the present. We often spend too much time stuck in the past or living in an imagined future when life is for experiencing right now. Centre yourself into the now. How do you live your life? In the past/ future/present or a mixture?
- Past/future/now. Think about what you did this morning, then fast forward to the future and imagine what you may do later on in the day. Now remind yourself that the present is the time that

matters most. Spend a few minutes 'in the now' recognising everything that is happening at this precious moment in time.

- Activity in the now. Think about what a moment is (2–3 seconds). Enjoy this moment before it disappears. Appreciate the next moment of time and notice how it is different from the last moment but still equally as amazing, unique and precious.
- Animals in the now. Visualise or move around the room imagining you are a tortoise / fish / lion / ant or bird. As you are carrying out this game, remember to be in the now.
- Connecting. The world is completely connected; everything is interlinked. Explore in your mind how you are connected to your class / school / town / city / country / world.

Repeat the above activity but with various members of your family including mum / dad / sister / brother / grandparents / cousins, etc.

- Wake up now. Lay down and close your eyes for a moment. When you open your eyes you are going to be more awake and alive than you have ever been. Tell yourself that 'when I open my eyes I will be totally in the now'. Spend a few minutes reinforcing this belief. Open your eyes and spend some time living in the now.
- Favourite music. Play a piece of your favourite music; absorb yourself into the music. When your mind wanders, refocus on the music. Pay particular attention to how the music makes you feel. What sounds do you hear? What patterns of sound, the beats and rhythms.
- The raisin. Give each child a raisin. The focus of this activity is to observe everything about the raisin with a focus on things you have never seen before, such as colour, texture, smell and feel. Spend a few moments just looking at the raisin; notice five things about it that you have never noticed before. Imagine what the raisin will taste like, visualise before tasting, then spend some time chewing slowly and noticing things that you have never noticed before. How many different things have you noticed? How amazing were you at spotting different things?

Repeat but this time drinking a glass of water, noticing the sensation, the feeling of the water moving down into your stomach. Enjoy its purity.

Reference: *Mindfulness Meditation for Everyday Life* by Jon Kabat-Zinn (2001).

- Feelings. Sit and think about how you are feeling right now at this precise moment in time. Describe the emotion to yourself; why do you feel like this? Has the feeling changed as you think about it? Why are you feeling like this; do you know the reason behind the feeling?
- Lovely me. Listen to your body and enjoy the sounds and beats it makes. Spend some time focusing on your heart beat, your pulse, enjoying your own smile and finding your glow and spirit within. Visualise yourself and enjoy the image. Notice and feel the warm glow of your body, around the outer edge of your body.

Spend some time thinking about the actual space your body takes up in a room, house, school, village, county, country, continent, world and the universe. Remind yourself this is you, living and experiencing things right now.

- Slowing down – stop revving like a car. This activity is about slowing down and spending a moment doing so. Think about a car at the traffic lights with the driver pressing the accelerator and revving the engine (wasting energy and overheating the car). Humans have a tendency to be like this and it's not helpful. Listen to your inner 'revving' and spend some seconds slowing down, unwinding yourself and taking the proverbial foot off the accelerator pedal.

Adults – when you come across a red light while driving, don't sigh but smile – turn the next few moments into positive ones and stop revving the car and yourself.

- Rhythm breathing. Spend a few minutes listening to the breath. At first it will be irregular in its beat. While you are listening to the breath, listen out for a rhythm to the breath; hear the sound in your mind. Turn the volume up on this sound.

- Clouds. Keep your attention focused upon your breathing. If thoughts come into your head, simply let them float away like clouds. Don't try too hard to push them away. Just let them come and go of their own accord.
- Let it go. The aim of the activity is to let any problems fly away. Imagine your worries are written on a bright red kite. Imagine releasing the kite and watch it fly up high into the sky and letting it go.
- The space within me. Try these abstract mind-focusing activities.

  - Focus on the 'space' between your eyes.
  - Focus on the 'space' between your ears.
  - Focus on the 'space' between your shoulders.
  - Focus on the 'space' between your elbows.

By focusing on the concept of 'space' you focus your concentration and yet relax your mind.

- Movement focus. This activity works well with all children, especially those who are developing the skill of sitting still.
- On the move. Choose a simple activity such as walking around a garden or the school playing field. Ask the children to focus on their left arms as they walk in silence.

During the activity ask them to be conscious of that arm, how it moves, how the muscles feel or whether it's hot or cold.

- Walk around the room without talking to anybody and notice the sensations or warmth as your feet touch the carpet. Move the focus to the contact on the floor of your toes, heel and ball of your foot. Moving around the room, notice the sensations in your legs and other body parts.
- Moving meditation. You are a tiny seed in the ground. Warm, feel the earth and the rain. You slowly start to grow… be aware of each part of the plant growing. Now revert back to a seed.

- Move around the room as the following things: a bubble / feather / pillow / jelly baby / star / leaf / tortoise / stream and fish.
- Walking breath meditation. Try synchronising your breathing with walking unhurriedly in the same motion or rhythm.
- Centring the balance. Stand naturally, lean forwards a little, backwards and sideways to develop a sense of how your body is balanced. Think only about your perfect balance and how it works.
- Shake it off.

  - Sitting on the floor cross-legged, shake arms and shoulders.
  - Stretch legs out in front of you while sitting down.
  - Stretch out toes and stretch out calves, then thighs.
  - Gently shake legs together.
  - Rotate both ankles in circles eight times.
  - Repeat in other direction.

- Toe tapping.

  - Heels together, tap top of feet together (count to 100 mentally).
  - Touch toes.
  - Hold arms out to sides, gentle breathe in and touch toes, withdraw to starting position while breathing out.
  - Repeat 3 times.
  - Focus on palms.
  - Hear your breathing, right hand on chest, left on lower abdomen (3 minutes).

- White light. Focus on the white light between your eyes – focus on this imaginary light above your eyes. Try to think only about the peaceful white light.

Thinkpoint: In books on meditation our 'wide awake' (conscious) part of the mind is often said to be like a chattering monkey – it is called 'the monkey mind'. Why do you think this might be so? If you could choose other animals, plants or things from nature to compare the mind to, what would they be and what are the reasons for your choice?

- Colour of the rainbow. Look at a picture of a rainbow. Talk to the pupils about enjoying the beautiful colours of the rainbow. Go through the individual colours from the top of the rainbow to the bottom, focusing on each colour, saying the colour to yourself and filling your mind and body with the individual colour. Link each colour to a feeling and notice the change in your body, e.g. red – warm, orange – alive, yellow – in the now, green – feeling heavy, blue – feeling cold and purple – feeling very secure.

- Nature observations. Spend a few minutes looking at these objects separately and in your imagination absorb their characteristics and qualities – try this activity with a rose, ice cube, flower head, fruit, colour pattern, clock face, vegetable or animal.

- Pool. Sit and imagine a circular pool of water in your mind. Imagine the pool being utterly still, without a ripple to disturb the surface. Find yourself thinking of nothing but the smooth surface of the water. Gently bring your attention back to the pool when it starts to wander and think about other things.

- Candle. Observe a candle for 1 minute. Close your eyes and focus on your breath; open your eyes and observe the candle. Repeat by imagining the candle (or you can use another object). Observe the object for different periods of time and at different distances from you. Focus on the second hand of a clock for 2 minutes. When your mind drifts, gently return it to the focus.

Thinkpoint: The skill in these activities is recognising when the mind has wandered off to be thinking about something else and gently bringing your attention back to the task or focus. During early stages of meditation the mind will wander off all the time, drawn in by other distractions. The skill is not to get annoyed at this fact but recognise it and return to the thinking focus. Discuss with the children how easily we can all get distracted and how we can then bring our attention back to the focus.

RELAXATION SKILLS IN THE CLASSROOM AND HOME

This section focuses on relaxing the body. Learning to relax is a life skill and an increasingly more important one at that. Today's learners are more successful if they are not tired or stressed out. Learning to relax not only aids sleep and recharges the battery but also gives you more energy to approach challenges in a more positive and energetic frame of mind.

The following activities can be used in the classroom at certain points during school time or at home to aid sleep or just chill out after a long day. The sleeping activities later on in the chapter are particularly useful due to the growing problem of child (and adult) insomnia which has worsened due to a whole host of reasons including more stress at school, increased screen time and changes to our diets and exercise patterns.

These relaxation activities ideally last for one to 8 minutes depending on the time of day and the purpose of use. Unlike meditation the pupils can lay down during the activities but teachers should be aware that after lunch children might fall asleep, which is usually to be avoided. Teachers can buy numerous pre-recorded relaxations for children which contain music and audio. The following activities work with some gentle music playing in the background and the adult guiding the children (or themselves) through the relaxations. As you become more experienced you can help the children visualise new ideas in the relaxations and ultimately create your own relaxations with the children. (See Figure 3.7.)

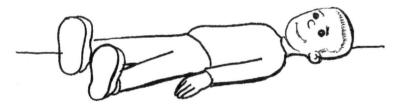

Figure 3.7 Relaxation

- Tense or relaxed? Spot the difference. This noticing activity highlights the different feelings of being tight or tense compared to being relaxed. It is important to recognise the two different feelings or states and why it feels better to be relaxed rather than tense or on edge.

Highlight before the activity that this exercise is all about noticing: being aware of a change in a feeling and being able to precisely pinpoint the exact moment when the feeling changes.

Squeeze two fists tightly together and then release the grip, noticing the exact moment when it stops feeling uncomfortable and starts to feel calm or relaxed. Discuss with the children the different feelings and why it feels better in one state than another.

Repeat with the following activities.

- Squeeze knees together – then relax or release.
- Crunch up toes and then release.
- Push tongue to the top of the mouth then release.
- Shut eyes tightly and then release.
- Purse lips together – release.

- Music: Listen to different styles of music (classical/jazz/rock). Notice how the music makes you feel; decide which style of music helps you relax. This activity highlights the difference between calm and upbeat while developing an understanding that sometime we need to be still and calm.
- Making-a-face relaxation. Relax all parts of your face. Spend some moments grimacing and tensing the different facial muscles (with eyes closed if you're going to get embarrassed!). Choose different facial muscles that you can relax.
- Calm photos. Look at some relaxing photos; these may include waterfalls or sunsets. Transport yourself into the photo and notice the effect on your body and emotions these have on you. Why do these photos slow us down? Take this opportunity to explain that having a rest or re-charging our bodies is a good thing as we are better at learning and tackling challenges when we are refreshed and ready to go.

- Muddy feet. Breathe correctly; stand with legs hip width apart. Close your eyes and imagine your feet are sinking into thick warm mud. Try to lift your big toes, now small toes. Keep the others still. Lift your leg out of the mud; imagine you are placing the leg into a bowl of warm water. Repeat with the other leg. How does it feel?

Relaxation time

Breathing. Spend a few moments gently breathing before starting these relaxations. Frame instructions to the children in this way…

Tell yourself you are going to spend some time relaxing, recharging your body for a few moments. Starting with your head, moving down to your toes, relax each part of your body by calming and stilling the muscles. As you relax the muscles and body parts think warm and heavy as you gently relax your whole body. Notice this lovely warm feeling you have created around your body; enjoy this feeling of relaxation. Be aware that even if you wanted to move you couldn't as your body is contented and relaxed.

- Floating. Lay down and start with some gentle breathing. Notice the warm feeling of lying down; be aware of the connection your body is making with the floor or bed – notice this warm contact. Tell yourself you are going to spend a few moments relaxing. Imagine you are a raft gently floating on the sea. You are safe; it is warm as the sun is out. Spend a few minutes enjoying this peaceful floating feeling. (See Figure 3.8.)
- Flying. Lay down and start with some gentle breathing. Notice the warm feeling of lying down. This time imagine your body feels very light and relaxed; magnify this feeling. Scan your body from head to toe, filling your body with a gentle light feeling. Close your eyes and imagine yourself being so light that you start to float upwards; it's a pleasant feeling. Notice as you gently continue to rise up and up through the ceiling and up into the clouds. You are safe and can open your eyes and return to the floor at any time. Enjoy this light floating experience. Spend a few moments enjoying your floating journey.
- Gentle flowing river. Spend a few minutes breathing in for 3 seconds and exhaling for 5 seconds. Lay down and start with

Figure 3.8 Floating relaxation

some gentle breathing. Notice the warm feeling of lying down; be aware of the contact your body is making with the floor or bed. Imagine you are lying on a raft gently floating down the river. Enjoy this calm feeling. What do you see and hear? You are safe and can open your eyes and return at any time. Enjoy this flowing river experience.

Thinkpoint: Why does it feel better to be calm compared to be being stressed? How precise are you at noticing the difference? Can you change how you feel? Are you better at learning feeling tense or relaxed? Why? How can you change how you feel when you are learning new things that are tricky?

- Sleep activities. These activities enhance sleep. It is also advisable to follow these simple rules to aid sleep.

  - Avoid screen time up to an hour before sleep.
  - Avoid food and drink up to an hour before sleep.
  - Create a night-time routine and stick to it.
  - Have a warm bath and story before bedtime.
  - Lavender helps calm the mood of the room.
  - Play calm music in the bedroom.

- Whale breathing. This type of breathing is excellent for calming down and falling asleep. Imagine you have a hole at the top of your head like a whale has (its blowhole). Breathe through this hole and imagine the air moving right through your body from head to toe. Breathe out through your toes. Breathing in through your toes, bring the air through your body in the opposite direction. Repeat four times.

Focus on different parts of the body and as you breathe out imagine any tension flowing away from these body parts.

- Heavy stone. As you lie in your bed notice the 'feeling' of your body resting on the bed. You may notice a warm feeling around the main contact areas, e.g. head, back and legs. Change the feeling to a heavy feeling pulling you deeper into the bed. Finally imagine your body and that the heaviness is coming together in a ball. Tell yourself this is a relaxing feeling and that you feel secure and safe. Finally imagine your body as a large heavy stone which is strong and secure, gently falling to sleep.
- Body relaxation. Focus on all your body parts starting from your toes and moving up to your head. Every time you breathe out you will feel more relaxed. Tense each area first then relax each body part slowly moving upwards. Scan your body for areas of stress; stop at any area of pain or stress. Slowly breathe out, removing the stress from that part of the body. Move on to other parts of the body that are tense or uncomfortable.
- Countdown 300. This activity stops the chattering monkey in your conscious mind hijacking your relaxation. By preoccupying your conscious mind with counting you can let your subconscious mind think about relaxing. Lay down and start with some gentle breathing. Notice the warm feeling. Tell yourself you are going to spend 10 minutes or so relaxing. Your subconscious mind is going to scan and relax your body: programme yourself to do this while you are counting slowly down from 300 to 0. If you lose count pick up from where you think you lost count from.
- Stairs. You are going to walk down ten steps into a calm garden. Every time you take a step, you will feel more and more relaxed. Notice the change as you move through each step. Be aware of a deep sinking feeling as you descend the stairs, further relaxing

you with every step. When you reach step ten you are totally relaxed.

Repeat the above but visualise a special garden at the bottom of the steps. Explore the calm and relaxing garden. Be aware that an incredibly calm feeling is circulating your body.

- Film of the day. Imagine a mini camera is in your mind; it has filmed everything you have done today. Play the film in your mind from the moment you woke to this final moment now as you are ready for sleep.

ENERGY RELAXATIONS

- Battery. Imagine your body is an empty battery cell. Gently breathe in new life to your battery. Feel with every breath the energy coming into your body. Feel the re-charging sensations in your hands, arms, chest, legs and head. Chose a colour to represent a fully charged battery as that vitalising colour flows through your body. (See Figure 3.9.)

Figure 3.9 Battery recharging

- Shower burst. Imagine yourself in a shower with the warm water flowing onto you. Spend a few moments noticing the warm water refreshing and invigorating your body. Experience the energy flowing into your body from the warm sparkling water. (You can always complete this relaxation actually in the shower.)
- Open door. Picture yourself walking down a long corridor. At the end of the hallway is a large oak door. You know when you open the door a whoosh of light will be released onto your body giving you a burst of energy and 'oomph'. Slowly approach the door; you are safe and this will be a wondrously warm and refreshing feeling. As you slowly open the door feel the power of the light re-charging your body.
- Warm glow inside. Gently rub your hands together until you experience warmth in your palms. Tell yourself that you are creating a glow that will warm up and give your body energy. Keep gently rubbing your hands and notice as the colourful glow moves up your arms into your chest and slow energy spreads into your body as you keep rubbing your hands together. Be aware how awake and rejuvenated you feel. It's a great energy boost to help you through the day.

VISUALISATIONS THROUGH RELAXATION

The use of visualisations through relaxation techniques has many benefits. These include an increased ability to internalise awareness, increased concentration span, greater control of thoughts (with associated ability to deal with negative thoughts) and increasing ability to create more detail in imagined scenarios. This creates more 'raw material' for writing and also enriches the experience of reading. In the classroom visualisations are an ideal tool for developing story ideas as it is a deliberate use of the imagination. Teachers often use pictures of the pupils' story ideas to help the children start the writing process. Visualisations can be used in the same way.

Visualising a story plot will help 'writers' block' by sparking the creative imagination into life which helps children during the writing process. In contrast visualisation is often used by top sports men and woman as way of experiencing victory ahead of time or playing through the match in the mind before a ball has been kicked or the starting whistle has been blown. (See Figure 3.10.)

- The tunnel. Ask the children to send a few minutes calming the breath and have some gentle relaxation music playing...

  Imagine you are walking along a calm beach when you discover a tunnel at the side of the ocean. As you approach the tunnel a warm glow descends across your body; it is an uplifting sensation. You enter the tunnel and various things appear that float by.

  (At this point tell the children that they are safe and whenever they open their eyes they will safely return to the start of the tunnel.)

  Things to visualise in the tunnel; animals, different colours, story characters, different story setting, a jungle, forest, plants, shapes and patterns, noises, seasons, trees, smells, objects that make you feel safe/amazed/sparkling.

  When running the activity again, ask the children to think of some different ideas.

Figure 3.10 Visualising

- Music meditation. Play some gentle instrumental music and suggest to the children that they can just let the music flow through their mind, putting aside any thoughts it might conjure up. Then ask them to see what pictures, stories, thoughts and images appear when they listen.
- A great place visualisation. Create a pleasant place in your mind, somewhere to go to feel inspired with energy and amazing ideas. What is this place called? What colours and smells does it hold? How does it make you feel?
- Leaf on tree. Imagine you are a leaf on a tree. Notice how you move in the wind and change colour as the seasons change. Watch the leaf fall during winter and fly across the sky. Where does it go? Who do you meet?
- The orange. Show the child an orange. Ask the children to close their eyes and visualise the fruit in their mind. Spend a few minutes slowly peeling the orange paying careful attention to details (smell, touch, taste).

Ask the children to visualise different smells and create that smell in their mind, e.g. a rose, a sweet smell, chocolate, grass, a flower.

As above but with different sounds/tastes/senses.

- Self-remembering. Think about yourself and how you have grown and developed over the years. Choose five different times in your life (some young, some older) and picture yourself in detail what you look like. How have changed?
- I love that book. Think about your favourite storybook and replay the story in words and pictures in your mind. Amaze yourself at the detail you remember.
- Space. Tighten your seat belt. You are on a rocket and heading into space. Feel the thrust of the rocket engines as you are catapulted into space. What do you see? What happens when your journey has just begun?
- He who dares wins. Think of a time when you have been brave and faced a huge challenge. Decide on a new challenge for yourself in the future. It could be riding a bike, learning to swim

or winning a race. Imagine yourself overcoming the challenge and achieving your goal. What does it feel like?

- Write your own. Encourage and guide the children towards writing their own guided visualisations. Ask them to think about the setting and theme as well as the correct word choice, selection of metaphors and careful use of punctuation to control the pace when the script is read aloud.

RELAXATIONS TO BOOST SELF-ESTEEM

These are simple but powerful strategies that can enhance pupils' self-esteem or merely give them a dose of confidence or security. The activities are ideal for pupils facing difficult challenges. They have been particularly successful in the run-up to Year 6 SATs and have stopped pupils losing confidence or 'wobbling' beforehand. Ideally you would use these strategies at least six weeks before the test to ensure they have maximum effect.

- Special place for the special one. Sitting down, think about your special place, which can be real or imaginary. Where is the space? What is in the space? Colours? Objects? Does anyone else know about the space? Importantly why is it special and how does it make you feel? Think about that special feeling it gives you. Where is that feeling in your body? Try to pinpoint exactly where the feeling sits. Enjoy and savour the feeling. Open your eyes. Try to recreate the feeling while sitting at your desk or when you need to feel safe or reassured.
- Anchoring finger thumb. Anchoring is a way of remembering or recreating a feeling. The trigger to remember this feeling is by simply squeezing the thumb and middle finger together on your right hand. Practise squeezing your thumb and finger together to establish an anchor or memory. The following visualisation will lock the anchor to the memory, which can then be recalled at any time to recreate a good self-esteem-boosting feeling.

Close your eyes and press your thumb and finger together to establish an anchor. With your eyes closed, in your mind's eye create a black and white photograph of when you were having a fantastic time, a truly memorable experience. This may be a birthday party, a holiday, a hobby – the only thing that matters is that the occasion is special to you.

With your eyes still closed, keep looking at the photograph of yourself having a great time and now enlarge it – zoom in to make it ten times bigger. Now turn the photo to colour and look closely at the scene. Look at your face and remind yourself why you were so happy. Look at everything that is framed in the photo. All the time keep your finger and thumb pressed together creating the memory anchor. Now transport yourself into the photo as if you were back in time at the occasion. Notice what it feels like; enjoy every moment of being there. After a while slowly open your eyes and release the thumb and finger anchor lock. By locking this happy memory into your anchor you can recall the feeling every time you use the anchor by squeezing your thumb and finger together.

Children can use this strategy any time they are feeling unsure – before or during a test or when they are feeling unconfident.

- Mountain. This activity is about feeling safe and secure by using the relaxation of a mountain to help you feel strong and confident. The idea of this relaxation is that a mountain is strong and immovable and by visualising that you are a mountain this sense of security will spread across your body and mind.

Sit on a chair and gently breathe in for 3 seconds and slowly out for 5 seconds. Put both of your feet together flat on the floor so they are compact and steady. Position your body so that you are sitting still, balanced and ready to turn your body into a mountain. Close your eyes and visualise a mountain: you are going to turn your body into a mountain and enjoy the strength and power of being such a great thing.

Imagine your legs are the lower half of the mountain, your body the middle of the mountain and your head the peak or tip of the mountain. Spend a few moments enjoying and feeling the solid stability of actually being a mountain. Nothing can move you or hurt you. Take strength from this feeling. Enjoy the magnitude of its power. While keeping your feet flat to the floor notice what plants are growing at the base of the mountain and what animals might be living there.

Spend a few minutes doing the same for the rest of the mountain. Continue looking at your mountain-self through the different seasons. Retain the feeling of strength of the mountain and revisit the security of the feeling by simply placing two feet together on the floor when required either at school or at home.

Repeat the above but this time as a tree or a lion.

- Special jumper. Do you have a favourite jumper? What does this jumper look like? Why is it special? Either imagine or actually put on your special jumper, noticing how warm and secure it makes you feel. How else does it make you feel? You can always remember this feeling and use it when you are down in the dumps.

- Being invisible. Imagine what it feels like being invisible. You are free to walk and think all by yourself. What a warm and amazing feeling! Enjoy the extra control you have but remember not to misuse your special power.

Repeat but this time being a fish, seahorse or dolphin.

- Smiling activity. Because smiling makes you stronger, spend some time developing your best smile in the mirror. Share it with your friends. Notice the warm happy feeling it gives you.
- Laughter all around. This is an excellent group activity. Laughing out loud in a group spreads an infectious buzz of energy and wellbeing. Spend some time practising your best laugh. As a group everyone should spend a few minutes laughing together. You will be amazed at the sense of togetherness and fun this creates.
- Magic stones. This activity works best in a classroom. Collect a bag full of differently coloured and shaped stones. Ask each child to select a stone that stands out to them or seems special to

them. Ask the children to study the stone; they should remember every detail including the size, shape colour and texture.

Now ask the children to hold their stone in their hand and gently squeeze it. Tell them to notice a warm feeling coming from the stone; this is magic coming from the stone. Explain to the pupils that their stones are special and will give them strength and courage when they need it. There are various relaxations that you can develop from using the stones.

Hold the stone and notice the warm feelings moving from your hand spreading to the rest of your body giving you confidence and strength.

Hold the stone in your hand and notice the magical colour coming out of the stone and giving you confidence and the ability to try new things.

Hold the stone and visualise an adventure while holding it. Try to think of lots of different ways the stone helps you to do this.

- Favourite character. Spend a few moments thinking about your favourite sports star, musician, super hero or film star. Pretend to be that person. What does it feel like? Imagine being that star in action (running, playing an instrument or dancing). Repeat with a person you know and admire. Think about what special quality they have – put yourself in their shoes to solve a learning problem you may have.
- Positive Chanting. The use of Positive Chanting is an excellent way of conveying positive messages about oneself. Essentially you repeat the positive phrase half a dozen times to focus the mind on a positive thought pattern. Another approach is knowing that the mind can easily fill up with negative thoughts so the use of a powerful and repetitive phrases help to promote self-esteem and a feel-good factor. A simple starting point is to replace each negative thought with a positive one. Whenever a negative thought appears in the mind, 'catch yourself' doing this and simply replace it with a positive one.

Examples of some Positive Chants:

- I will be happy.
- I feel great.
- I've done this before I can overcome this challenge.
- I love myself and I'm proud of my achievements.
- I believe in myself.
- I feel strong inside.
- I will go to sleep.
- Keep learning.
- Resilience is my friend.
- I'm going to stick at it.
- Visualise being stuck – coming out the other side.
- I like being stuck; it means I'm going to learn something new – hurray.

CHAPTER 4

Jumpstart mindfulness and reflectiveness

Everything should be made as simple as possible – but no simpler.
(Albert Einstein)

WHAT IS MINDFULNESS?

This section builds on earlier meditation activities by highlighting the idea that mindfulness is like 'ongoing meditation'; paying closer attention to everything you do and realising that life happens now, in this present moment. Reflectiveness of oneself involves 'stepping back' to take some time for introspection. It is closely linked with learning from experience – thinking about what happened, what you did and what can be learned from the experience, including what you might do differently next time. Thus it is about actively making meaning in your life, which in turn contributes valuably to a deeper sense of purpose. Preliminary activities pave the way for exercises in reflective writing. This is where children look back at an event, for example, to think about it from different perspectives and what learning value it contains.

An influential figure in the world of mindfulness over the past few decades is Jon Kabat-Zinn, Professor of Medicine Emeritus and creator of the Stress Reduction Clinic and the Centre for Mindfulness in Medicine, Health Care and Society at the University of Massachusetts Medical School. His book *Full Catastrophe Living* (1990) is still widely regarded as a classic text on using meditation and mindfulness to promote health and wellbeing. Kabat-Zinn also defined what he sees as the seven elements or pillars of mindfulness. These are: non-striving, non-judgement, acceptance, letting go, trust, patience, and beginner's mind. They can be imagined as seven overlapping circles, each being a part of the others and each contributing to the whole.

- Non-striving does not mean ceasing to work towards greater achievements. In many areas effort and competitiveness are both necessary and desirable. The word is also linked to 'strife', however, indicating that at times striving becomes an unnecessary struggle that brings anxiety, frustration and disappointment. The notion of non-striving in mindfulness is simply to be fully present in the moment; enjoying the actual experience of your life by letting moments unfold without being drawn into thoughts of the past or the future. The ancient saying, 'Sitting quietly, doing nothing, spring comes and the grass grows by itself' captures the essence of this idea.
- Being non-judgemental involves a heightened sense of acceptance; an acknowledgement of the reality of things, noticing with a degree of 'friendly curiosity' as life unfolds. It also means being more compassionate about oneself, letting go of regrets and self-criticism. Non-judgement does not mean the absence of a view of the world, nor giving up our considered opinions or of condoning what we know to be harmful or evil.
- Acceptance goes hand in hand with being non-judgemental. In terms of our experience of life, both good and bad things happen. We can acknowledge the inevitability of this: we can perceive our experiences without needing to judge them as good or bad. Experience is experience. This does not mean being 'resigned to our fate' or ceasing to make plans for the future or giving up on the desire to better ourselves. The philosopher Alan Watts summed up the notion of acceptance vividly when he said that living one's life is a bit like being a cat falling out of a tree – we can't prevent the fall, but we can choose which way we orient ourselves while it happens.
- The notion of letting go fits well with Watts's metaphor. Letting go in the context of mindfulness means not losing ourselves in the stories our minds continually spin, being trapped in what the writer Robert Anton Wilson (1999) calls 'reality tunnels'. The idea here is that 'I am not my thoughts', but something more essential and profound. Thoughts can be imagined as clouds drifting through the sky. We can watch them come and go

without trying to stop them, judge them or resist them. By extension, we can also let go of our resistance to reality. The cat is falling out of the tree and no amount of struggle will alter that.

- Trust here means trust in our own deepest experience and in our sense of who we really are, rather than buying into the yarns that our minds can spin about ourselves. The Victorian poet Gerard Manley Hopkins wrote about the notion of 'selving', of 'going oneself' (in Gardner 1970), by which he meant embracing our uniqueness as it is expressed through the process of life and all of its experiences. Kabat-Zinn (2009) adds that trusting our intentions and our desire to be happy and freely ourselves is an important aspect of this element of mindfulness.
- Patience contributes to and is defined by the other elements we've looked at. In mindfulness patience means 'taking a break' from always trying to get somewhere, influence somebody, make something happen, striving towards greater success. It implies ideas we have touched upon earlier such as co-operating with the inevitable, taking time to 'be' rather than 'do', and realising that all too often things can only unfold at their own pace.
- There is a saying that 'in the beginner's mind there are many possibilities, but in the expert's mind there are few'. Cultivating beginner's mind includes being curious about the nature of the mind itself and the thoughts it produces. It involves looking at things in different ways as well as endeavouring to experience life directly by removing the mental and emotional 'filters' that colour our perceptions. The educationalist Margaret Meek (1998) writes about how young children experience the world with a sense of 'firstness' – everything is fresh, unique, filled with wonder as they explore with boundless curiosity (if we let them!). Beginner's mind is also about us too approaching the world anew, with that sparkling sense of firstness.

In summing up, then, mindfulness like meditation is not about success or failure, competition or comparison with others. It is not about doing nothing, giving up or in any way deadening the mind. It is the very opposite, allowing us to wake up to the freshness and beauty of life by deliberately paying attention to the present moment without being influenced by the mind's incessant chatter. Furthermore mindfulness as we advocate it in this book is not religious. Though it has its roots in spiritual traditions, here we present it as a pragmatic set of ideas and techniques that help to develop children's creativity and wellbeing. Practising meditation and mindfulness activities also encourages patience and persistence, two key elements of the resilience that children – that all of us – can benefit from in so many areas of our lives.

TALKING OF VALUES

The values we hold powerfully influence the way we regard ourselves and other people, and yet all too often we 'absorb' values from parents, friends, from books, films and the TV: the culture we're embedded in transmits its values to us in a multitude of ways, often subliminally. So an important part of the task of raising wellbeing is to explore values consciously so that we can make up our minds how we want to be.

- Prompt the children to ask themselves 'What's important to me?' They can list as many things as they like, and then if it's possible put them in order of significance. Are there any things that most or all of the children feel to be important?
- Discuss various meanings of the word 'value' with the class. The online dictionary www.etymonline.com informs us that circa 1300 value meant 'the price equal to the intrinsic worth of a thing'. From the late fourteenth century the sense had shifted to 'the degree to which something is useful or estimable', which in turn stems from the Old French meaning worth, price, moral worth, standing or reputation.

Help the children to question the definitions given. For instance, can the intrinsic worth of a thing always be calculated? What examples can they think of where worth cannot be measured? What links exist between something having intrinsic worth – worth in itself – and price? What does 'moral worth' mean? What might be the connection between 'worth' and 'worthy'? In what different ways can something be valuable? Are there any links between the values we hold and the notion of something being valuable?

- In P4C (Philosophy for Children), enquiries often stem from a consideration of concepts such as freedom, loyalty, truth, identity, happiness, love, power and justice. Discuss first what these words mean. Ask the children if they consider all, some or none of these to be values. Do any of the children think that one of these ideas is more important than any of the others, and if so why? Are any of the ideas linked, and if so how?
- Get children to explore their values further by asking further questions such as: Would you rather be poor but happy or rich but miserable? If you could become much more intelligent, but to do so meant that you would never see your friends again, would you do it? If a wizard said that by magic he could give you ten extra years of life but that somewhere in the world someone you never met would die as a direct result, would you take him up on the deal? (Would this be a good wizard by the way, or a bad one?) If you knew that your friend was cheating in an important test, would you tell on him/her? What if the person was someone you knew but were not friendly with? What if the person was someone you disliked?

A great little book full of teasers like this is Gregory Stock's *The Kids' Book of Questions* (2004). He's also done one for adults too (1987) – see Bibliography.

- Present the class with some proverbs. Ask the children to think about which values are being expressed in them and to what extent they agree or disagree. As a preparation for this, encourage children to question what certain words might mean, for example in our selection – fault, good, wise, grasp (in what sense?), richest, knowledge:

  - A fault confessed is half redressed.
  - A good name is better than riches.
  - A heavy purse makes a light heart.
  - All's well that ends well.
  - Better to be happy than wise.
  - Do as I say, not as I do.
  - Exchange is no robbery.
  - Grasp all, lose all.

- He is richest that has fewest wants.
- Knowledge is power.
- Live and let live.
- No gain without pain.

See also the chapter on values in Bowkett and Percival's *Coaching Emotional Intelligence in the Classroom* (2011).

SEEING THE GOOD

An important aspect of meditation and mindfulness is the realisation that 'I am not my thoughts, I am not my feelings.' That is to say we are all more than our thoughts and feelings. We have the ability to stand aside from them and watch them come and go, realising they are parts of a much greater whole.

Another technique is to think creatively and view apparently negative thoughts and feelings in a more positive light. The idea has been called the Principle of Positive Purposes. A good example is if you put your hand on a hot surface. You immediately feel pain and snatch the hand away. The pain itself was unpleasant, but it served the positive purposes of getting your hand out of the way quickly to minimise the damage, and perhaps make you more careful in future where hot surfaces are concerned.

Similarly emotions that we normally regard as unpleasant can convey a positive message. Sometimes the message is obvious and sometimes it requires some reflection. So if for example Steve or Kevin feel frustrated if a piece of writing is not up to what we regard as our usual standards, we can acknowledge the frustration as an indication of our desire for higher standards. If we feel disappointed that a publisher has rejected our manuscript, the 'energy' driving the feeling can become a sense of determination not to give up trying to succeed. By the same token, anger can highlight an underlying recognition of unfairness or injustice; guilt or shame might remind us of our sense of morality; envy can act as a reminder to look again at what we truly value in life.

- Work with the class to come up with a list of unpleasant/ negative feelings then help the children to apply the Principle of Positive Purposes. This can be done 'in the abstract', as we've done it previously, although children may choose to recall particular occasions when they actually felt the emotion you're working on. Bringing the feeling component into the activity can make it more powerful and beneficial – though again we advise that if any child feels uncomfortable doing this, he or she must be allowed not to take part.
- Positive opposite. This is an effective technique for modifying persistent negative thoughts. If through various other activities you have taught the children how to notice their thoughts and feelings more readily they will master this technique very quickly. The idea is to notice an unpleasant thought as it occurs and to immediately think of a positive opposite. So as soon as a child notices anger he (or she) deliberately thinks of being calm. As soon as he notices envy he thinks of the good things he already possesses and/or wishes the person who sparked the envy good fortune.

This technique stops the 'drip feed' of negative thoughts that can develop into an ongoing attitude. Over time the negative thoughts may occur more rarely or, when they do appear, have much less of an emotional charge than in the past.

REFLECTIVE WRITING

At its simplest reflectiveness is the capacity we have to think things through. Self-reflectiveness is the process whereby we use introspection to examine our thoughts and feelings, our beliefs, values and purposes in life. This is often done while in a quiet state, one where we are able to notice our thoughts – both conscious chains of reasoning and deliberation and sudden subconscious insights that allow us to forge new links of meaning. The outcome of any act of reflectiveness is a new understanding sometimes as the result of a changed perspective on things. The whole aim of being reflective is to grow and flourish as a human being.

The fruits of reflectiveness are often expressed through writing (though this isn't essential). Reflective writing can take many forms and can combine the creativity of new insights, as already mentioned, with a degree of analytical and methodical thought that can lead to fresh conclusions and new decisions upon which we can act.

Showing children how to practise reflectiveness in the classroom brings a number of important benefits for their broader learning:

- A better understanding of personal strengths of weaknesses.
- An increasing ability to know how to act upon personal weaknesses.
- A deeper understanding of values and beliefs.
- A more acute recognition of assumptions on which our beliefs may be based.
- A more frank acknowledgement of worries and fears.
- A more flexible and creative approach to solving problems.

Several of the activities in this book would serve as precursors to more fully developed reflective writing; see for example 'Observations of nature without judgement' (p. 8) and 'Keep a moods journal' (p. 44).

- In a sense children already practise reflective writing when they write stories that require some crossings out and changes of mind. Extend this good working habit by asking children to rule a line vertically down the pages they are going to write on, so creating two columns. Have them write only in one column, leaving the other blank for now. Once they have completed a piece of work (first draft or polished), after a day or two ask them to re-examine it and write any observations, errors noticed, phrases and sentences that please them, etc., in the other column. Point out that if they have noticed *any* area where they can improve then their learning has progressed. Also, highlighting pieces of writing that children are pleased with, especially if they can say why they have impressed themselves, indicates deeper insight into language and the writing process.

- Present moment statements. The teacher, poet and scholar Thich Nhat Hanh (pronounced 'Tick Naught Han'), in his book *Present Moment, Wonderful Moment* (Hanh 1993), encourages us to reflect on what he calls 'verses' that amount to simple statements recognising the obvious but amazing fact that we are alive *now* as we go about our ordinary everyday business...

  - I feel the chair supporting me as I sit here to write.
  - I am walking and look, my legs know just what to do.
  - Outside and a cool gust of wind tugs leaves from the trees. I watch them spinning.

Note that these are more than just observations; they are recognitions of being alive in the present moment. Because such verses are plain and simple, most children will easily be able to write their own and gain the double benefit of reflecting on the act of composition as they write, and repeating the verses to themselves whenever the moment matches.

Extend the work by inviting the children to write 'myku' poems based on their reflections (see the section 'Observations of nature without judgement' on p. 8 for more details). These short, simple pieces challenge children to choose words carefully...

Ravens,
windy day –
flutter like leaves.

Anger –
I notice it
rise and fade.

New day.
So much change –
But I'm still me.

Once children become more familiar at creating and using such statements, they can try something a little more philosophical...

I am looking at my hand. Is it the same hand I had when I was born? Will it be a different hand in my old age?

The rain helps the grass to grow. The sun turns the water to clouds to make more rain. I tilt my head up and feel the drops on my face. Grass, sun, clouds, rain and I are all part of the same thing.

I have finished my meal. Where did the food come from? Who do I thank?

- The Japanese poet Matsuo Basho, who lived in the mid-to-late 1600s, combined brief, clear moments of perception and appreciation expressed in simple verses with more detailed prose descriptions of the places he visited and the people he met (a style known as *haibun*, the combining of poetry and prose). His purpose – apart from simply exploring and enjoying the world – was to draw life's deepest meanings from the most ordinary day-to-day events (reference: *The Narrow Road to the Deep North*, Basho 1966). So, for instance, a child's written account of an end-of-term trip to a theme park might be accompanied by a short verse in the Hanh style – 'Just as the roller-coaster plunges down the thrill rises in my chest. So many ways of feeling alive.'

Reflective writing attempted at this modest level helps to develop a skill that can be practised at a much higher degree of sophistication. For example, Monash University in Melbourne, Australia, offers an online language and learning course with advice to students on how to apply reflective writing both to their assignments and more generally to themselves as they work towards their degrees and their chosen career beyond (www.monash.edu.au/lls/llonline/writing/medicine/reflective/index.xml).

OTHER ACTIVITIES FOR DEVELOPING REFLECTIVENESS

Whereas meditation is a way of calming the mind, stepping back from our thoughts and even endeavouring to still conscious chatter entirely, reflectiveness is a way of using our ability to think to reach greater awareness and understanding. While these two mental activities are different, they complement one another such that meditation can be used as a way of reaching the state of mind where reflectiveness can occur.

- Presuming meaning. Pictures, pieces of music and objects (natural or made) can all be used to stimulate reflectiveness. Whatever the aim of the reflection, *presume* that the thing you have chosen carries meaning that will help the outcome to be of use. So if for instance I have a problem to solve and I choose to reflect on an apple, I presume (or pretend) that somehow the apple will help me to solve the problem. (You will appreciate that any work you do with the children on boosting their creativity will be useful here.)

Remember that reflectiveness uses both subconscious assimilation of ideas and conscious 'thinking through' or working out of an issue. Often a subconscious insight that suddenly 'pops into mind' can set off a chain of logical and methodical thought that might lead to a solution. Similarly, conscious thinking 'feeds back' into the subconscious to enrich the network of associations that are built up around the matter being addressed.

If you think yourself or the children will find it difficult to presume meaning, use Tolkien's idea of suspending disbelief. To get the most out of *The Hobbit* we hold back our disbelief in dragons and elves: to get the most out of the object of reflectiveness we hold back our disbelief or scepticism that it can assist us.

Note that in some spiritual traditions linked with meditation and reflectiveness (Zen for example) we are advised that things 'are as they are'; that they have no meaning in themselves and that any meaning is ascribed by the human mind. A central aim of meditation in these traditions is to 'de-conceptualise' the world, to free the mind such that it perceives reality directly. The technique of presuming meaning is not antagonistic to such spiritual practices but rather is yet another potential ability our mind possesses.

- Reflective listening is a strategy that arose from the work of psychologist Carl Rogers. It was initially used in the context of client-centred therapy but has much wider applications. Reflective listening involves the following.

  - Really focusing on the conversation you are having and cutting down on distractions as much as possible.
  - Accepting the speaker's viewpoint without necessarily agreeing with it. In other words, avoiding the impulse to prejudge, resist or reinterpret the view of the speaker.
  - Feeling calm and comfortable in the speaker's presence and allowing him to feel comfortable in yours. Some calming breathing or meditation beforehand can help achieve this. Obviously, feelings of animosity or dislike inhibit reflective listening.
  - Summarising what the speaker says in your own words, giving the speaker opportunity to correct any misunderstanding on your part.
  - Responding to the particular point that the speaker makes, rather than jumping to another point or going off at a tangent in your reply.
  - Feeling comfortable with the 'thoughtful silences' that may occur during a reflective conversation of this kind, presuming that when the speaker falls silent he is giving your words sincere and serious consideration, and vice versa.

Schools that run P4C (Philosophy for Children) programmes will recognise that this model closely resembles the ethos of listening and mutual respect that we aim to achieve during an enquiry. Peer coaching sessions also incorporate these aspects of reflective listening.

These various means of developing reflectiveness all build towards the more general habit of reflective learning. Reflective learners develop the attitude of considering how new knowledge and skills relate to present progress and desired future outcomes. A quick and simple way of getting children to do this is by encouraging them to ask the following questions.

- What new things have I understood?
- What have I got out of this / how will it help me?

In this way learning is linked to action and ideally the motivation to continue actively learning.

Reflective learning is underpinned by a number of insights:

- That the learner must take a share of the responsibility for personal growth. (Realising that 'life is what you make of it' – a cliché, but true.)
- Working to see a clear connection between the effort the learner puts into an activity and what he gets out of it.
- Valuing the learning experience by reflecting on why the learner is doing it and what's in it for him.
- Continuing to 'learn how to learn' by adding new skills to the learner's repertoire.

Note: The educationalist Alistair Smith has written a number of books on learning to learn under the banner of Accelerated Learning (for example, Smith 1998).

JOURNALING

This is the habit of keeping a journal that explores thoughts and feelings around the events that happen in one's life. It is different therefore from a diary that routinely records the things we did, people we met, etc. The aim of journaling is to reflect on oneself and our relationships with others. And while entries in this kind of journal can be upbeat and relate to pleasant experiences, the full benefits of the practice are felt when using it to deal with stress, anxiety, anger and other negative emotions.

One key aspect of journaling is to write about the issue concerned in detail. In explaining the technique to the children, reassure them that this is not about 'raking over old ashes' or wallowing in unpleasantness that may be happening now. The point of keeping such a journal (apart from getting things off one's chest) is to solve problems and so improve matters. It's also important for children to understand that their 'thoughts and feelings books' will be completely private, unless any child chooses to show it to someone else. Also, children must be told that (for once!) spelling, punctuation and grammar are not important. What matters is that children express themselves as fully as possible with the aim in mind of feeling better about things and sorting out their problems. (If any child has difficulty writing to the extent that it would make keeping a journal impossible, suggest the options of audio recording, having a 'journal buddy' to transcribe, drawing the problem in detail, or a combination of these.)

With all that said, if any child simply doesn't wish to write about any issue or doesn't want to keep a journal at all, then that's fine. The techniques we mention in this book will work for some children but not others.

If you want to introduce journaling as an option in your classroom, here are some tips.

- Set aside a little time each day for the children to write; 10 to 15 minutes is fine. If some of them don't wish to put anything in their journals, suggest quiet reading or some other kind of writing such as a story.
- Remind the children that neatness isn't paramount. Also encourage the children not to 'self-censor' and just let the ideas come out.
- You can offer the suggestion that children write just on one page of the journal and leave the facing page blank. This can be used later for further reflections, new ideas, or to comment on what was written earlier.
- Reinforce the fact that if any children get upset as they write, they can stop, have some quiet time, talk to someone or all of these.

- Another technique is to give the journal a double purpose. One half can be used for exploring and dealing with problems while the other half is used as a 'gratitude journal' where children record the good and pleasant things in their lives and/or a 'goal-setting journal' where they enjoy creating big visions, writing about their aspirations, sources of inspiration and practical steps they can take towards what they desire.

TAKING RESPONSIBILITY

Responsibility is largely about 'response-ability', the ability to respond appropriately. It is an important aspect of developing wellbeing since it draws together self-esteem, honesty, fairness, a degree of trust in others and trustworthiness in oneself, clear-headedness, independent and creative thinking (i.e. reflectiveness), kindness, compassion and forgiveness. (A useful jumpstart precursor activity would be to ask children what qualities they think a responsible person possesses.)

- In terms of children becoming more responsible offer them a 'code of honour' which might include the following.

  - Keeping your word. Once you've said you'll do something, do it (ideally without needing to be reminded) as soon as you can.
  - Reflecting on what it means to 'do the right thing' in given situations.
  - Doing something with commitment and determination once you've agreed to it. Doing your best.
  - Being prepared to face the consequences of your actions. These consequences can be good things, especially if you've acted responsibly; but if they're not, have the courage to admit mistakes and make amends.
  - Thinking things through before you act (where this is possible; sometimes we need to decide on the spur of the moment).

  Discuss the benefits of being a responsible person and the disadvantages of being irresponsible.

- Use examples of ethical dilemmas to give the children the opportunity to probe more deeply into what responsibility entails. We have recommended Gregory Stock's *The Kids' Book of Questions* (2004) elsewhere, but it's also useful in this context.

You can extend this activity by incorporating different 'what if' scenarios into your chosen dilemma.

For instance, a classical ethical dilemma is where ten people are drifting in a life raft having abandoned a sinking ship. The raft cannot hold any more people without sinking. An eleventh person swims up to the raft, utterly exhausted, and begs to be taken on board.

What would you do?

– What if the person in the water was a convicted murderer?
– What if one of the people in the life raft was a convicted murderer?
– What if one of the people in the raft told the others he was going to die from illness in three months' time?
– What if you knew that one of the people in the raft had always been greedy and selfish?

Ask the children to think of some what-ifs of their own to enrich the discussion. Explain that their scenarios do not need to be realistic; even fantastical ideas can be useful. For instance, what if you could become invisible whenever you wanted to?

On the other hand there are always issues in the news that generate often heated debate across a wide spectrum of opinion. Having picked which issue to focus on, one useful and interesting angle is to ask children to consider these two questions.

– What do you think would be the responsible thing to do?
– What would you personally do?

Children do not need to 'go public' with what they would personally do if it's not a responsible course of action; the aim of the activity is for children to assess for themselves how responsible they are as individuals and how this meshes with what they understand the concept of being responsible to entail.

SELF-ACCEPTANCE

Meditation, mindfulness and reflectiveness all encourage an appreciation of the small and ordinary things in life; of other people and of our day-to-day experiences, aiming to cultivate an attitude that is the polar opposite of the culture of materialism that can and does lead to so much unhappiness in the modern world. If fame, money and status are the things by which we largely or wholly measure our success, then most people will be forced to conclude that they are not successful.

We have seen that an important step in the development of wellbeing is the insight that 'I am not my thoughts'. By the same token, 'I am not my feelings' and 'I am not my possessions'. While these contribute to our experience of life we can recognise that in essence we amount to more than them. Try this thought experiment. If you lost a possession, even one that meant a lot to you, would you be any *less you* as a result?

Of course you might regret the loss of the thing and be saddened by it: you'd miss it, but that's different from saying that you have lost a part of your essential self. By the same token, if you change a negative pattern of thought or modify unhelpful feelings (as we hope this book has demonstrated that you can), then were the negative thoughts and feelings 'more you' than the positive ones you have now? We can also ask in this context, which thoughts are more real? We still have that sense of 'being me' whatever thoughts and feelings come our way.

One element of self-acceptance then is to accept the notion that the thoughts, feelings and things in our lives are not our essential selves. We are more than the sum of our parts. Some children might find it difficult to agree with or even understand these ideas. Introducing them to other notions and concepts in this book might help, as would running philosophical enquiries in the classroom (see www.sapere.org.uk for an introduction to philosophy for children). When children can think more deeply and searchingly they are more able to tackle abstract and subtle ideas and relate them in practical ways to their own lives.

Other useful ideas that build towards self-acceptance include these.

• Feeling comfortable with yourself, realising that no one is perfect. Reflect on the fact that some people spend fortunes on trying to stay looking young and beautiful, though inside they might feel unhappy or afraid that their good looks will inevitably fade, or envious of the younger and more attractive people they see around them.
• Recognising personal strengths and weaknesses. This doesn't imply that we shouldn't try to improve in whatever ways we can. Taking action to address weaknesses where this is possible and exploiting strengths in ways that are beneficial to ourselves and others raises self-esteem and contributes to a sense of wellbeing.
• Using imagination to create an overview of life. All of us surely can think back to some unpleasant time in our lives, but realise now that life is a process of learning and development and that what happened a) is past and b) can be reflected upon to add something useful and positive to the way we live now. A greater vision is to see our individual lives as tiny things that are all too fleeting. Meditating on the idea of cherishing every moment (because there is not an endless supply of moments) offers a perspective that can prompt us to act for the good.
• Avoiding comparing ourselves with people who are somehow 'better' or trying to make ourselves look better by being critical of those who are less successful, wealthy, attractive, etc. Comparisons like this are the opposite of self-acceptance.
• Doing something positive for others. This can be the smallest act of kindness or consideration, but each time we act it has a positive influence on our lives and makes it harder to hang on to the idea that we are 'no good'.

According to the psychologist Albert Ellis (2006), the highest aim of self-acceptance is to accept oneself unconditionally. If we impose conditions on how, when and where we accept who we are, then should we fail under those conditions we risk the backlash of self-doubt, recrimination and criticism.

MAKING A DRY LANDSCAPE GARDEN

These are also called Japanese rock gardens or Zen gardens (Zen being a method of reflection around the question 'who am I?' and experiencing the world directly with a quiet mind, uncluttered by thoughts; the word 'Zen' derives from the Sanskrit for 'meditation').

While such rock gardens can be created outdoors, miniature versions are easily made in the classroom and need be no larger than an exercise book. Traditionally they are made using gravel and rocks, though children might also choose sand, fish tank gravel, shells, twigs, pebbles, crystals and beads. Water can be simulated using small mirrors: traditionally in Japanese rock gardens running water is represented by wavy lines raked in the gravel.

Looking at pictures of dry landscape gardens online you will see that in the main they are rather sparse and unfussy, even apparently random. (An article in *New Scientist* magazine for September 2002 reported a claim by Japanese scientists that visitors to the Ryoanji Temple garden in Kyoto unconsciously detected a tree pattern in the arrangement of stones that was pleasing to the eye [Young 2002].)

While traditionally there are many rules governing the creation of these gardens you need only suggest to children that the ones they make shouldn't be too 'busy', that they should be good to look at and created in a quiet state of mind. While the stones in Japanese rock gardens are not symmetrical, neither is any attempt made to 'simulate nature', that being something of a contradiction. Children are free to create symmetrical patterns if they wish however. Also suggest to children that when choosing objects for their gardens, the aim may be to create something that is just aesthetically pleasing, or has meaning, either for the individual or that carries more general symbolism. Either way, one purpose of making a garden is to remind children that even the small and simple things in life can be appreciated.

The page opposite gives some ideas from children we've worked with.

'I put in this little glass ball. It's a paperweight, but to me it means trying to see things clearly and trying to see beyond what's on the surface.'

'I used some shells I collected when we went to the seaside. Every time I look at the rock garden I'm reminded of my holiday.'

'I made a little circle of pebbles, one for every pet I've had since I was a baby.'

(Coincidentally, just after visiting this class Steve saw the movie *Mr Holmes*. At the end an elderly Holmes – played by the actor Ian McKellen – made a circle of stones to represent significant people in his life who had now passed on.)

'The wavy lines I raked in the gravel remind of me the ups and downs in life. The lines are not broken because life goes on anyway.'

'I put these beads in my garden because my friend Kirsty gave me a necklace but it broke. I didn't want to throw it away though. Kirsty is pleased that I kept the beads and used them like this. When we look at them we remember that we are still good friends.'

'I used these shells. We had just read Ted Hughes's poem "Relic". Our teacher explained it was about the way nature works. We had a discussion on whether life was just about eating or being eaten, or whether there was more to it than that.'

'I made the stones look random because really you never know what is going to happen in your life.'

As you see, all of these children thought carefully about which objects to choose and in some cases how they were arranged.

Here are some further suggestions if you want children to make dry landscape gardens in class.

- Spend time explaining what Zen gardens are and how they link to the work you've done with meditation as part of your wellbeing programme. Show the class some pictures of actual gardens.
- Many children will want to bring in their own objects to form part of their gardens; however, it's an idea to have some boxes of shells, stones and so on handy as well as supplies of fish tank gravel and sand. Rakes for the sand can be sharpened pencils, combs cut to short lengths, or children can use their fingers. Decide beforehand what you will use as the bases for the gardens. Squares or rectangles of stiff cardboard or hardboard are fine, as are picture frames (minus glass).
- Explain that when the children create their gardens they should do so mindfully – being fully aware of and gaining pleasure from every moment of the activity; the feel of the objects, the slow careful raking of the gravel or sand, the way that the garden takes shape, etc. That is the main purpose of the activity.
- Each child should make his own garden, although you might decide to have some children working in pairs. Avoid large groups. Children should concentrate on their own work and not be distracted by their classmates. You need not insist on absolute silence (friends working together may want to discuss their project), though the atmosphere should be calm and peaceful – the making of a dry landscape garden is a meditation in itself.

As children finish their work, have them sit down and either write about their experience or read quietly until the last garden is finished. Ideally there shouldn't be a time limit on the activity though obviously during a busy day you may have to impose one. It's important however that children shouldn't feel rushed and should come away from the work feeling that their garden has been completed.

Photograph the gardens when they are finished: you can use the pictures subsequently either with other groups to introduce the Zen garden project, or with the same class as a stimulus for further discussion. If you or the children want to keep a garden you can mix the sand with some PVA glue and a little water just prior to laying it down – obviously children need to make their patterns in the sand quite quickly before it hardens. Otherwise, the gardens can be dismantled once photographed and the general materials used again. (There is a Tibetan Buddhist tradition of creating 'sand mandalas', complex designs using coloured sand which are ritually dismantled after completion, this act representing the transient nature of all things.)

CHAPTER 5

Jumpstart being well

> Never be in a hurry; do everything quietly and in a calm spirit. Do not lose your inner peace for anything whatsoever, even if your whole world seems upset.
>
> (Saint Francis de Sales)

This chapter will draw together ideas and techniques from the previous sections while offering new activities to help children gain more of an overview of their lives. There will be an emphasis on reflective writing, plus looking at stories that highlight values and morality. We also explain how wellbeing can fit into the home or the school structure and how it impacts the whole school and isn't just an 'add-on' to an otherwise busy curriculum.

THREE IDEAS TO JUMPSTART WELLBEING

1. Do something worthwhile today

Not long ago Steve was at a supermarket thinking about how glum the girl at the checkout was looking. She was unsmiling and to all appearances seemed tired and bored, pushing items across the laser reader like a robot – until the lady in front of Steve said to her, 'I like your earrings dear. Did you get them locally?'

Immediately the girl's whole manner changed and her face lit up. She paused to touch an earring, thanked the customer for noticing and then chatted briefly about where she bought them, feeling pleased because she got them in a sale. She was still smiling minutes later as Steve walked away from the till.

The point is that small acts of kindness and politeness can lift someone's mood and cast their whole day in a better light. Compliments when they are given need to be appropriate and sincere of course, though there are many other things we can all do to make ourselves and the people we meet more cheerful. Appreciating someone's good idea, paying them the respect of listening, saying 'you're welcome' when someone thanks you, helping out even in small ways all help to establish the atmosphere of the classroom.

2. Gathering treasures

This is a reflective activity that invites children to think back to times when they have felt inspired or pleased with their achievements; when they have been paid a compliment or done something positive for someone else; when they laughed at a joke someone told or were simply in a good mood for reasons they can't now remember or were unaware of at the time. If children practise gathering treasures as part of their journaling work then they can glance back over past pages to remind themselves of the positives in life and thereby influence their present mood.

3. A treasure box of ideas

This works well as a classroom project. The idea is to have a box where children's good ideas can be placed. These could be good ideas for stories, a sentence a child has written that works well and one that he is prepared to share, an idea for a class display or topic, a fund-raising idea... Introduce the idea by showing the class the treasure box and reading out a few good ideas, either ones you have made up or that children have previously mentioned. Explain that the aim is not to try to fill the box quickly or for children to compete with each other, but that it's important for them to feel that their thoughts are valued. Build regular visits to the box into the classroom routine – once every week or two is fine – and either pick out an idea at random to talk about or put into action, or sift through until you find one that is particularly interesting, topical or fun to do.

On the next page are ways to take this further.

The word 'treasure' comes from Latin and means 'a storehouse, repository or collection'. (Interestingly it shares the same root as 'thesaurus'.) There are many variations of this activity.

- Ask the children to recall occasions when they felt good about themselves for whatever reason. If they wish they can share these memories with classmates or just note them down so that they won't be forgotten.
- Make a display of clippings from magazines and newspapers about acts of kindness, courage, etc. These can be combined with 'gee whiz' facts about nature, from science and so on that help to cultivate a sense of wonder and appreciation of the world.
- We've already mentioned the value of collecting inspirational quotes. You might consider having a space in the classroom for 'good words of the week', making some time to discuss them.
- Create a 'treasure box of good ideas' and invite children to contribute. Ask them to write their ideas for stories, for discussion topics, book reviews, suggestions for poetry you can read to the class, etc. Make the reviewing of some of these a regular class activity.

TIME-PATH VISUALISATION

Visualising is one aspect of metacognition, the faculty we have to notice, reflect on and manipulate our own thoughts. Practising meditation greatly improves children's ability to do this, given that it develops powers of concentration and turning the attention inward. It also helps children simply to let thoughts come and go without them being a distraction, or to reflect on certain ideas to explore them more deeply. This in turn creates the opportunity for new insights, reinterpretations and resolutions.

While we looked earlier at the value of 'present moment awareness' – fully appreciating the experience of being alive in the here-and-now – creating a visualisation of one's journey through life also contributes to a sense of wellbeing. There are several ways children can do this.

- Begin with a short relaxation/meditation session, then ask the children to imagine that our lives can be thought of as lines or paths and that in a moment they will have an idea of what theirs looks like. It may seem like a thread, a ribbon, a road, a country track and so on. If it's more like a thread or ribbon, instruct each child to notice where he is – in the present moment – in relation to the rest of the line, which represents his past and his future... Are you beside the line or on it? Does it pass through you? What shape is it as you notice it reaching backwards and forwards in time? Make it clear that you are not asking children to have any memories from the past nor to see pictures of an imagined future. *All* you want them to do is visualise the life path and how they relate to it.

There is a balance to be struck here between giving children enough information to do the activity and being too prescriptive about what they will imagine. Ideally children will notice a spontaneous image of the life path and themselves here-now in relation to it. During a workshop session one boy produced the drawing in Figure 5.1 for us.

Figure 5.1 Time-path visualisation

When we asked the child if he knew what it meant he nodded, smiling. 'I have lots of good memories from when I was younger. I carry them under my arm where they're close. And on the other side the future goes up and gets wider. I think that's about being able to choose from lots of different options.'

On a note of caution, some children might not have such a positive experience. Either negative memories start to come up or unpleasant feelings linked to non-specific thoughts. As we have advised elsewhere, any children who start to feel uncomfortable can stop the activity at any time. Afterwards, give them the opportunity to do some calming work or another activity where they can gather positive thoughts to feel better about themselves.

- Subsequent time-path sessions focus on working more deliberately with the visualisation. If you want to concentrate on the past, ask the children to imagine the path as a strip of film. Anything that is unpleasant is now visualised as 'fogged out' sections of film, while anything positive can come more clearly into focus. If children want to, they can 'step into' these positive sequences and enjoy those memories all over again. (Such memories might be ones that a child can always recall, though some may have been forgotten and now just pop into mind.)
- If working with future intentions, again ask children to imagine the path as a strip of film and to see clearly the good and worthwhile things they would like to experience and achieve. Some children may notice that the time-path branches in more than one direction. Extend the activity by giving children strips of paper to draw and colour their future paths.
- Thinking metaphorically. Subconscious imagery – ideas that come 'out of the blue' – can be symbolic rather than literal, as in dreams. It's not essential that children understand the meaning of the things they imagine: what matters is how they feel about the thoughts. Negative material can be worked on and hopefully resolved while imagery that is accompanied by pleasant feelings can be nurtured.

One way of helping children to understand these concepts, and to develop their ability to work with metaphor, is to have them draw a 'life-story string' such as the one in Figure 5.2.

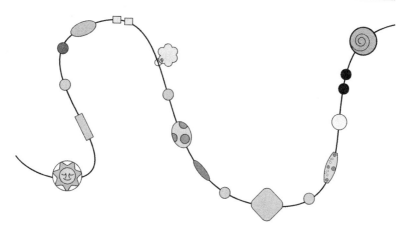

Figure 5.2 Life-story string

First, discuss with the class the notion that objects can stand for certain feelings and ideas. Go through some examples, together with phrases and sayings that clarify the point: 'She has a sunny disposition', 'He's always been my rock', 'We can branch out in all kinds of directions.'

You or particular children may then decide to work on the future only. In this case, they must visualise or draw an object that allows them to feel good about themselves *now*. You can talk to them beforehand about which objects could represent determination, looking forward to the future, feeling confident, etc. Then the children 'string together' a number of such objects in their minds (they can draw the life-story string beforehand to make visualising easier). Instruct them to see the objects as clearly as they can. If there are sounds associated with any object, ask children to 'turn up the volume'. Encourage them to handle the objects to enhance the tactile element of the visualisation.

Most importantly, encourage the children to notice and savour the good feelings that come along as they use their imaginations in this way.

MEETING YOURSELF ALONG THE WAY

Another technique that uses the time-path visualisation involves imagining that you can meet up with your younger or older selves. This is in not in any way mystical; rather it is just another use of the imagination to tap into subconscious resources, based on the principle that 'we know more than we think we know'. Here are a few ways of running the activity.

- A pleasant place. Work with the children over a series of relaxation/meditation sessions. As part of the activity ask each child to visualise a pleasant place where he can feel comfortable and at ease. Encourage children to imagine such a place in as much detail as possible using colour, sound, smell and textures so that it is really vivid. Ask them to allow positive feelings to become associated with this place.

Once the visualisation is established, children can add objects of special significance or ones that have sentimental value. These will live on in the imagination even if the actual object no longer exists.

A younger or older self can now visit the special place to meet the child in the present. The 'now-self' can offer ideas or comfort to a younger self, while an older self can be a source of wisdom and advice. Children might have clear memories of what they looked like in the past, though if they don't it won't affect the beneficial effects of the visualisation. Similarly a child might have only the vaguest idea of what he could look like when older. What's important is that he has a sense of the *presence* of the older self.

Once this has been achieved, the visualisation is most effective if the child doesn't try to put words into the mouth of the older self. This might sound odd, but the aim is to draw on subconscious resources to gain new insights or make fresh connections. Sitting quietly with the attention turned inward, a child is more likely to have ideas popping into mind spontaneously than if he is making an effort to formulate them for himself.

- What would XXX say? Another technique is to invite another person to the pleasant place, preferably someone that the child admires. It might be a real person or a fictional character. Again, the aim is to draw on information and networks of association existing at a subconscious level, allowing them to become conscious now. This is the essence of creative thinking.
- Along the path. The pleasant place visualisation happens in the here-and-now, but another technique is to have children imagine that they can move along the time path. They may travel into the past – possibly just to revisit pleasant memories, or to join a younger self in their 'own domain'. (Steve remembers that when he was about six years old he trod on a caterpillar, not killing it but squashing one end. He tried to keep it alive in a matchbox but it died a couple of days later and he cried bitterly, always regretting that he'd killed it. Going through the visualisation of visiting younger-Steve, reassuring him that treading on the caterpillar was an accident and reminding him that trying to save it was an act of kindness even now brings comfort. It's also a salutary reminder of how even the smallest and apparently insignificant experiences can have a powerful influence on a child's mind.)

Visualising moving forward along the time path allows children to create plans for the future, visualise goals and enjoy ahead of time the pleasure of those goals being achieved. In other words the child takes the opportunity to clarify a sense of direction and purpose, even if in reality he later changes his mind in light of new experiences.

A CLOUD OF QUESTIONS

This is a whole-class activity that takes just a few minutes each time you run it. Show the children an ordinary everyday object such as a pencil and invite them to come up with as many questions about it as they can during the given time. For the initial session they don't need to write anything down (though you might consider recording it if you want to do any analysis of the questions later). Point out that there's no 'hidden agenda' going on – the exercise is just about asking questions. Explain too that it doesn't matter if the children don't know any of the answers.

The purpose of 'a cloud of questions' is to shift the children's behaviour away from being passive recipients of knowledge (assuming that they are) towards becoming more active 'questioneers'. Subsequent sessions reinforce this and challenge the children to think more deeply about the questions they ask. Extend the activity by introducing the following.

- Asking the class to categorise the questions they've generated. Again, encourage as many ideas as possible. Categories can include:

  - questions that are easy / difficult / impossible to answer (with a reason attached)
  - questions that everyone / some people / no one already knows the answer to
  - subject, topic or genre specific questions
  - questions that have only one answer / more than one answer
  - open questions / closed questions.

- Using more abstract ideas rather than objects. Begin by getting the class to ask as many questions as possible about the concept of a 'fact'. In this case allow time for discussion of some of the questions. Incisive questions we've had in the past include: Who decides when a fact is a fact? Why do some facts change? Is a fact the same thing as truth? Can a fact be true and not true at the same time? Can something that is untrue be a fact? Can something that cannot be measured be a fact? If something can't be proved, could it still be a fact?

We're sure you'll recognise the benefits this kind of activity brings across the whole field of the children's learning. Further, when children 'take ownership' of their questioning in this way they become more confident and realise that enquiring is not so much an admission of ignorance as an active desire to find out more (we like to point out the similarities between 'questions' and 'quest').

- Using philosophical concepts such as loyalty, freedom, morality, life, justice, etc., as the starting point for the children's questioning. Again you might decide that setting aside time to discuss some of their ideas is fruitful.
- Showing the class some text that you know most of the children will find difficult to understand. Encourage them simply to ask questions about any aspect of the writing that puzzles them. Follow up by giving children the opportunity to research some answers (rather than you simply telling them the answers).
- Encouraging questioneering during topic work. This helps children to feel less daunted by technical terms and jargon, and diminishes the anxiety of looking foolish for asking a question.
- Being prepared yourself whenever the situation arises to say, 'I don't know, but how might we find out?'

A SENSE OF WONDER, A SENSE OF HUMOUR

In our opinion these two traits contribute significantly to anyone's mental and emotional wellbeing. We also feel that they go hand in hand; that they are mutually supportive and beneficial. Some of the world's most respected scientists, for example Albert Einstein and Richard Feynman, were noted for being able to see the funny side of things coupled with a childlike curiosity that led them to explore some of the universe's deepest mysteries. In the field of spirituality too statues of the Maitreya Buddha are usually shown laughing, while the philosopher and Zen scholar Alan Watts, especially later in his career, brought a sense of joy to his consideration of 'the meaning of it all'.

Most young children display a similar readiness to laugh, to delight in experience as well as an often insatiable curiosity. This way of looking at the world is the opposite of the seriousness, stress and anxiety and that can so easily darken children's lives as they grow older.

Cultivate the gifts of wonder and the ability to laugh as part of your wellbeing programme.

- Discuss with the children what it means to wonder about something. What could the connection be between wondering and something being wonderful? Check what 'wonderment' means. What is wonderful to you? What do you think 'a sense of wonder' might be, and what has it got to do with the other activities for wellbeing you've asked the children to do? What do you think it means to have 'a sense of humour'? Do you think a person can see the humorous side of things even if the situation is serious? What has humour got to do with the other things associated with increased wellbeing?
- Invite children to find and share a 'wow fact of the week', something that has truly astonished them. Create some display space for this. Ask others in the class to look up associated facts.
- Show videos and still images of the natural world; sunsets, oceans, skies, crystals, deserts, animals, plants… There are thousands of stunning examples online.
- Point out that even the everyday things that we normally take for granted are pretty amazing. Show them pictures of the inside of a smartphone for example and explain how it works – or get them to find out for themselves. Help them to understand how different foodstuffs come from all over the world. Tell them about how tea for example ends up on the supermarket shelf.
- Make some time for children to tell humorous stories, anecdotes and jokes. Grab some images of humorous notices you'll find online and make a display.

If you type 'what are the beneficial effects of laughter' into a search engine you'll see how much research has been done and is being done in this field. The benefits of laughter and lightheartedness are numerous. Tell the children about these.

Finally always remember, 'Start every day with a smile – and get it over with' (W. C. Fields).

NOBLE QUALITIES

We are using the word noble here to mean 'of high moral character': it goes without saying that in this context the idea has nothing to do with social status. Ordinary people in everyday situations can *aspire* to develop in themselves the qualities we are talking about – fair play, selflessness, courage, good faith, honesty and truthfulness being among the most important. (In the following section we look at the hero figure in literature, folklore and film. Typically such heroes will display the qualities above plus others. Anticipating this closer look, we feel that 'The Hero' is an archetype, an ideal template against which we can measure ourselves and our actions. The hero figure embodies what is good in human beings and serves as a reminder of what noble conduct means and implies in our lives.) We think it is important that children should not be lectured on the topic of noble qualities. A few, we hope, more elegant methods are suggested below. Having explored values and moral dilemmas, and given that meditation and mindfulness practice is a regular feature of classroom life, we feel that many children will appreciate the personal and social advantages of acting 'nobly'.

- Offer a definition of the words 'noble' and 'qualities' (various attributes possessed by someone or something: also a standard when measured against things of a similar kind). Ask the class to list what they think are good examples and why.
- Explore these qualities further. For example, in looking at 'selflessness' you might ask questions such as; What is the opposite of selflessness? Does the word suggest 'being less of yourself'? What are some examples of selfless behaviour? If I do things just for myself sometimes, is that being selfish? What is 'the self' anyway? Is 'my self' everything I am and everything about me? If I'm not bothered about being rich or famous, but I don't help other people much, am I being selfless? If I did become rich and famous and helped lots of people, does that make me more selfless than if I was poor and just helped a few people?
- Ask the children to think of occasions in their own lives when they felt they were being selfless (or honest, truthful, etc.). If children are happy to do so, have them recount the experience (pointing out that this is not bragging).
- Encourage them to reflect on these qualities further by giving some hypothetical situations. If by not telling the truth I avoided hurting someone's feelings, would that be the right thing to do? If I discovered that my friend had tripped and sprained her

ankle, would I help her to get home? Would I still help if it meant missing a movie at the cinema that I had already paid to see? If I helped my friend and she didn't even thank me, would I help her in the future? Would I help someone I didn't like if he or she had sprained an ankle in the same way?

- Ask children to look for news items that illustrate real-life examples of noble qualities.
- Use quotes and aphorisms to consolidate the children's understanding of the noble qualities...

> 'I look only to the good qualities of people. Not being faultless myself, I won't presume to probe into the faults of others.'
>
> (Mahatma Gandhi)

> 'Courage is rightly esteemed the first of human qualities... because it is the quality which guarantees all others.'
>
> (Winston Churchill.)

> 'Many individuals have, like uncut diamonds, shining qualities beneath a rough exterior.'
>
> (Juvenal, Roman poet)

> 'It is not enough to have great qualities. We should also have the management of them.'
>
> (Francois de La Rochefoucauld)

THE HERO TALE

So-called hero tales have been around for thousands of years and most likely exist across all cultures. The folklorist Vladimir Propp suggested that the hero is one of seven basic elements of narrative (the others being villain, problem, journey, partner, knowledge and power, and important object (reference: *Morphology of the Folktale* 2001). Another researcher, mythologist Joseph Campbell, was consulted by producer George Lucas in conceptualising what became the Star Wars sequence of movies. Lucas's aim was to create 'a myth for the twentieth century'. Significantly, the Star Wars films have been among the most popular ever made. (Towards the end of his life Campbell reflected on the importance of myths with regard to the human condition. He felt that one factor in the difficulties affecting modern Western culture was that the West had become 'demythologised'. He was also of the opinion that young men especially could lose their sense of direction in life because in most cases they were not initiated into manhood as youths in traditional cultures were for many centuries. See for instance Campbell's *The Way of Myth* (1994) and *The Power of Myth* (1988) for a much greater exposition of his ideas.)

Ironically the word 'myth' is now mainly used to mean something that is just fantasy, something that isn't true, while one online dictionary describes a hero tale as 'a piece of fiction that narrates a chain of related events' (www.thefreedictionary.com). We think this is unfortunate insofar as myths are not just inconsequential pieces of entertainment but stories that *tell us something true*: narratives that tap deep into the basic human need to make sense of the sometimes chaotic sequences of events that constitute human existence. Myths also explore the idea of high moral standards within the ongoing struggle between good and evil, implicitly asking us to measure our own conduct against that of the main protagonists. This is why stories have a resolution – a re-solution – a solving again of the problems that are an eternal feature of human existence. The ultimate objective of the hero is to overcome the villain and restore, for a while, harmony and balance in 'the mortal realm'.

Apart from creating contexts where the hero can show his or her noble qualities myths offer concrete examples of abstract concepts such as loyalty, justice, freedom, morality, identity and others that make up the fertile soil of much of philosophy, showing how they interact within the dynamic of human lives.

Myths also celebrate life as a quest, an adventure, something that has direction, purpose and meaning – adventure deriving from the Latin *adventurus* 'about to happen', from *advenire* 'arrive'. We think it's not a coincidence that we talk about someone's 'life story'. Campbell used to say to all of his students, 'Follow your bliss.

Doors will open where you would not have thought there would be doors.' (Apropos Campbell's advice, the careers' teacher at the school where Steve was a pupil used to tell the students, 'Find something you love to do and get someone to pay you to do it.' When he found out that Steve wanted to be a writer he added, 'But get a proper job as well.')

- Ask the children to pick a favourite book, film, comic, etc. Or you can offer examples such as Star Wars, Doctor Who, Batman and so on. When the children have a story in mind, ask them to think about how many of Propp's basic narrative elements it contains. Compare these modern stories with some of the great myths such as the labours of Hercules or Jason's quest to find the Golden Fleece. Discuss why stories that have the same basic structure have existed for so long. Why do the children think we need to have stories like these? (Go beyond what might be their first response of 'because they're fun and exciting'.)

Tip: Familiarising children with the basic narrative elements gives them a great planning tool when they are creating stories of their own. See Steve's *Countdown to Creative Writing* (Bowkett 2009) for more details.

Look at some of the qualities of 'the hero' in more detail.

- Courage. This is not about being fearless, but about acknowledging one's fears and acting responsibly anyway. Ask the children to think about any occasion when they have done this (children don't have to share their experiences if they don't want to).
- Flexibility of thought and action; being skilled in terms of considering the situation and making judgements and decisions that allow the hero to progress in the quest and that lead towards a resolution of the problem.
- Determination. This means having a clear vision and sense of direction and being prepared to work hard to get where you want to go. In many stories this amounts to defeating the villain. However, we can use the notion as a metaphor. The 'villain' might be our own fear of failure, or apathy, envy,

arrogance or any of the 'mean' qualities that are traditionally associated with the character of the villain.

- Sacrifice in the sense of being prepared to give up certain things in pursuit of what you value more. So if our aim is to learn to play a musical instrument we will have to make a sacrifice of time and effort to achieve this. Look in the news for examples of self-sacrifice. What did the people concerned have to give up? What did they achieve for themselves and/ or others?

- Resilience (from the Latin to rebound or recoil). Resilience means 'bouncing back' when things don't go our way. It also involves using failures and setbacks as positive learning experiences. So for instance when someone loses a game in sport, if they are resilient they will reflect on why that might have happened and be determined to have another go. Allied to this is the idea that part of the hero's quest *is to be tested*. In traditional tales there exists 'this world' – the world of our ordinary everyday lives – and 'the other world' of new experiences and challenges. When a hero figure sets out on an adventure, at some point he crosses into the other world. At this boundary between the known and the unknown we find the 'threshold guardian'. This might be a person or a situation that tests the qualities of the hero. Metaphorically the threshold guardian could be the doubts or fears that we harbour, which might otherwise prevent us from succeeding in our goal.

- Loyalty. At the heart of it, the hero is loyal to his mission, to his sense of purpose and vision. He is of course also loyal to the ones who support him, who wish him well on his way or who need his help.

- Responsibility – 'the ability to respond'. This again requires being able to look at a situation and to bring to bear the qualities of flexible thinking and good judgement (bearing in mind the old saying 'Good judgement comes from experience, and experience comes from bad judgement').

- Wisdom. The word includes showing good, sound judgement and discernment and derives from roots meaning 'to see' and 'to know'. Ask the children to think back to any occasions when they made a wise decision (or indeed an unwise one –

and what did they learn from that?). Interestingly 'wizard' comes from the Middle English *wys*, meaning 'wise'.
 – Bright spirit. This is a heroic quality in the sense of being animated, alive, actively relishing the adventure of life even when there are difficulties and setbacks. It arises from a combination of all of the qualities mentioned above and, if we might suggest this, allows the hero to shine.

• Make a class display featuring pictures of superheroes and ordinary people who have done heroic things. Intersperse these with brief descriptions of their deeds and the qualities that make up 'the hero'.
• Look at examples of villains from different stories and list the 'mean' qualities they have in common. Ask children to use what they find to create a villainous character of their own, either drawn or described in words.
• Ask children to use the circle diagram we looked at in the section on 'Outside world, inside world' (Chapter 1, Figure 1.2, pp. 3–6) to reflect on what heroic qualities they think they already possess? Do they also recognise any 'villainous' qualities in themselves? Again children need not share any of their thoughts on what is essentially a self-reflective activity.

ALL THE WORLD'S WISDOM

Once upon a time, Monkey decided that he would collect all the wisdom in the jungle and take it to a place where it could be safely kept.

First he made a bag of tough, dried palm leaves which could be fastened with a length of twine. Then he began his search, gathering up all of the knowledge and wise sayings that he could find. Most of the animals were pleased to help him, though Tortoise pointed out that the bag must be pretty heavy by now.

'I will struggle under the weight of this knowledge for only a little while longer,' Monkey explained. 'And then I will take it somewhere safe and leave it there, because wisdom, after all, needs to be preserved.'

Monkey worked hard at his task and soon had all the knowledge and wisdom that he could find. The bag was bulging with it. He looked around for a place of safe keeping and finally decided to put it at the top of the tallest tree in the jungle.

He tied the twine about his neck so that the bag nestled against his belly. Then he started to climb. It was tough going and he had to rest several times. As Monkey took a break on a stout branch high above the ground, Parrot noticed him and commented that the bag full of knowledge was going to be rather high up for some of the jungle animals to reach. 'Tortoise will never make it up there,' Parrot said.

Monkey shrugged. 'I can't help it if he's slow and not built for the job,' Monkey replied. 'Mine is a noble mission, I'm sure you will agree.' And he climbed on before Parrot gave him his answer.

Quite soon Monkey found the going very difficult indeed. The weight of the bag seemed to increase, and it constantly got in his way as he reached for the higher, thinner branches. Finally there came a point when Monkey felt that he could labour no more. The bag was just too much of a burden.

Just then he caught sight of a snail regarding him quietly from a leaf where he was sunbathing. Feeling the need to share his problem, Monkey explained what he was doing and how troublesome his task had become.

Snail listened patiently before answering.

'Well, I carry my container on my back,' he said. 'Perhaps if you did the same your job would be easier.'

And in that moment Monkey realised that he didn't have all of the knowledge and wisdom in the world at all, so he climbed back down the tree and released the contents of the bag back into the jungle, where he had collected them.

Questions to consider

1. Do you think that Monkey's mission was noble? Give a reason for your opinion.
2. If you could pick three ideas that you would want to put in the bag of knowledge because you think they need to be preserved and shared, what would they be and why?
3. Can you explain how the bag of knowledge and the tree in the story are metaphors?

THE TOWN BEYOND THE HILL

Once there was a hermit who lived on top of a hill. Down in the valley to the East lay a town and in another valley to the West a very similar town followed the winding track of a river. These two settlements looked identical to the hermit. They both seemed pleasant enough places. Maybe that was why people rarely, if ever, climbed the hill to visit the neighbouring town.

However, one day quite early in the morning, as the hermit sat on his front porch enjoying the sunshine, he noticed a lone figure labouring up the hill towards him. This person must have set out from the eastern town at the crack of dawn. The hermit followed the traveller's progress with interest, and eventually saw him to be a young man who, despite the effort of climbing, walked with a smile on his face.

Some time later the young man reached the top of the hill and arrived at the hermit's rough shack. 'Good morning sir!' the young man called.

The hermit returned his greeting, adding, 'You look hot and thirsty. Can I offer you some water to refresh you on your journey?'

The young man accepted this offer gratefully and the two sat talking for a while. 'I have decided to go and live in the town down in the western valley,' the traveller explained. 'I like the people in the town where I live. They are friendly and welcoming, but I want a new challenge in life.' The hermit thought this was very commendable. 'I have heard that the people who live there are also friendly and helpful. Is that right?' the young man asked.

'I'm sure,' said the hermit, 'that you will find them to be just as you expect.'

Soon afterwards, rested and refreshed, with a wave of his hand the young traveller continued on his way.

Now it so happened that just a few days later, as the hermit sat once more enjoying the view from his porch, he saw a second traveller climbing up the hill from the town in the valley to the West. The hermit watched with interest and soon saw that this walker too was a young man who, despite the clear air and sparkling sunlight, laboured with a sullen look on his face.

Eventually this young man reached the top of the hill and arrived at the hermit's rough shack. The hermit greeted him and offered him rest and refreshment, as he usually did whenever someone passed by. The traveller accepted gratefully and the two sat for a while and talked of this and that.

'I have decided to go and live in the town in the eastern valley,' the young man explained. 'I want a new challenge in life.' The hermit thought this was very commendable. 'I'm fed up with the folks where I used to live. They are miserable and bad tempered. Mind you, I've heard the people to the East are no better. Is that right?'

The hermit finished the last of his water and smiled. 'I'm sure,' he said, 'that you will find them to be just as you expect.'

Questions to consider

1. What do you think the story is trying to teach us?

2. How do you think the hill and the towns in the story could be metaphors?
3. Do you agree or not with the proverbs below? Give a reason for your opinion.
4. What do you think these proverbs might have in common?

- Smile and the world smiles with you.
- As you make your bed, so must you lie on it.
- It is a long lane that has no turning.

THE STORY OF WALKTALL

Walktall lived in the village of Koori, on the edge of the river, at the foot of the red hill. He was the son of Gubba Jack and Jalana, a fisherman and his wife. Walktall was a dreamer. He dreamed of the old times when the sky was new and everything was fresh and beginning. Back then, thought Walktall, wishes were real things like stones and trees and water. And what you wished helped make the world.

Walktall's greatest wish was not to be so tall. For you see, he was named for what he was. When Walktall stood up, the others in the village looked small beside him. And when Walktall walked, no one could keep up with him. The Koori children sometimes laughed at Walktall's great height and his long strides. This made him very unhappy, so unhappy that he would hunch his shoulders and pretend to be shorter. Yet the children still taunted him and laughed. But what could he do about it?

Nothing, Walktall, he told himself. Nothing.

One day Walktall had gone away from the village to practise with his boomerang. It was his favourite possession and he was very proud of it. To show that it was his, Walktall had painted himself upon it; thin and long, so nobody would mistake it for theirs.

Walktall stood by the matchwood tree and threw his boomerang with a strong, sure arm. It swirled away from him – swish-swish-

swishswishswish… And curved around the ochre rock and returned – swishswishswish-swish-swish.

Walktall caught the polished painted thing and frowned. He looked at the drawing of himself. You always come back to me, always the same, Walktall thought unhappily.

He threw his boomerang all through the morning. The sun rose higher and the shadows grew shorter, even Walktall's, though that meant nothing to him. At last, at the noonday, Walktall decided he had practised enough. He made one final throw, his finest of the day.

The lovely elegant boomerang spun away from him – swish-swish-swishswishswish…

And this time did not come back.

Walktall frowned a deeper frown. Perhaps the boomerang had caught in some branches. Or maybe it had clipped a stone and clattered to the ground. Or possibly some of the silly Koori children were teasing him again! Walktall decided to find out and walked after the boomerang with his long, loping strides.

He passed the ochre rock. He passed the stand of matchwood trees beyond. He passed the green pond and the long grass…

And found himself upon a dreaming track that he had never known about before. Gubba Jack had told Walktall about these paths that the ancestors had walked long ago. They led, Gubba Jack said, to many interesting places, though just where Walktall's father had not been able to say.

Since there was nothing much to do that afternoon, Walktall chose to follow the track and see where it went. Perhaps, he thought, to an interesting place. In fact it led straight and true to a huge eucalyptus tree. In the tree was a koala, shaded by the leaves and protected by the branches.

'Hai Koala,' Walktall called, smiling in a friendly way. 'I am looking for my boomerang. Have you seen it?'

Slowly the koala looked down at the boy. 'It came swishing past me not too long back. Went that way.' He pointed farther along the track.

'Thank you... Um, Koala, where does this track lead to, do you know?'

Slowly the koala nodded. 'To the best place of all to be,' he said in his gentle, cooing voice.

'I see,' Walktall said, not really seeing it at all. 'And Koala, a last question. Why do you just cling there in the tree, spending your time eating eucalyptus leaves?'

Koala pondered this slowly. Then he said, 'I like eucalyptus leaves. I like this tree. I am Koala.' And with that, he closed his eyes and slept.

Walktall went on his way.

Presently he passed by a warm shallow lagoon. There on a grey rock, sunning itself, squatted a gecko. It looked up at Walktall as the boy's shadow fell across it. Walktall knew that geckos were harmless. He made a small bow of respect.

'Hai Gecko. I am searching for my boomerang. Have you seen it go by?'

Gecko lifted a foreleg and pointed along the way.

'Follow the track,' Gecko said in his high clicking voice, 'and you'll find it where you want it to be. Now please, step away Walktall. You are in my light.'

Walktall promptly moved sideways so that the strong sunlight fell again upon the gecko, who stretched out to enjoy the warmth to the full. 'Why do you spend all day on the rock?' Walktall wondered.

'It is what I do and therefore what I am. I am Gecko. I live for the heat of the sun.'

Walktall made what he could of the answer, which wasn't very much, and went on his way.

Shortly afterwards the track took him up the side of a hill. From the top of that hill Walktall could see a village that was built along the curve of a river. Nearby, cracking its fleas in a busy way, sat a dingo. It regarded Walktall with sharp and clever eyes.

'Hai Walktall,' barked the dingo. 'I hear that you are looking for your boomerang.'

Walktall nodded eagerly. Something told him he was nearing the end of his search. 'Good day to you, Dingo. Yes, you are right. Have you seen it?'

Dingo lifted a dusty paw and pointed. 'It is down there in the village. Standhigh has it now.'

Walktall made one of his puzzled frowns. 'Standhigh? Who is he?'

'Oh,' said Dingo, grinning and showing his side teeth, 'you'll know him when you see him. He is about your size and he stands proud and upright. All the village people know him and respect him for what he is.'

Walktall's frown faded a little. 'Well thank you Dingo for your good advice... Um, if I may ask, why do you just sit and bite your fleas all day, when there's so much else to do?'

Dingo woofed with laughter. 'More for *you* to do, maybe. I am Dingo, and Dingo has fleas. I am what I am and that's all I can be.'

Walktall thanked Dingo for this puzzling reply, and strode down into the village.

To show that he meant no harm and was unafraid, Walktall threw back his shoulders and smiled in a friendly fashion. The people of the village responded with waves and smiles of their own. Walktall felt pleased.

He found himself walking through the village as though he knew his way around, straight to a hut at the far end and straight inside, where he found his boomerang lying on the floor.

Walktall picked up the boomerang and realised that Standhigh had come in.

'Hi Standhigh. I am pleased to meet you at last. I have heard a lot about you. Is it all true?'

'It's as true as other people wanted it to be,' Standhigh said. He shrugged his lean shoulders. 'But what really matters is what's true from now on!'

That made Walktall laugh, long and loud. And Standhigh laughed with him, just the same.

When the laughing was done, Walktall bowed to Standhigh in respect. Standhigh bowed also, for the same reason.

'I thank you for your wisdom, Standhigh. And do you know, this is an interesting place after all. I think I'll stay here!'

So saying, Walktall turned away from the mirror and strode out into Koori village, taking his boomerang with him, which had returned to where it had started from after all.

Questions to consider

1. What do you think these stories have in common in terms of their main theme?

2. This tale is a parable. Look up the word if you don't know what it means. What features does a story need to have to be called a parable?
3. Do you agree with Dingo when he says 'I am what I am and that's all I can be'? In what sense could that be true? Does it mean that Dingo could never change?
4. What does Standhigh mean when he says 'It's as true as other people wanted it to be' after Walktall wonders if what people say about Standhigh is true?
5. What does the ending of the story mean?

FORGIVENESS

This is a deep and deeply significant subject and one that we can only touch on here and then hopefully point the way forward to further learning – you might begin by seeking out *Forgiveness: how to make peace with your past and get on with your life* by Dr Sidney B. Simon and Suzanne Simon (1991; see Bibliography).

Our emphasis here is not so much how we might or should react when someone forgives *us*, but rather how we ourselves make acts of forgiveness and how these are essentially focused inwardly on ourselves rather than necessarily being directed explicitly to the person or persons we feel have wronged us.

In that regard forgiveness is 'a conscious, deliberate decision to release feelings of resentment or vengeance toward a person or group who has harmed you, regardless of whether they actually deserve your forgiveness' so that we can live with a calm heart and a clear mind. Essentially when we forgive in this way it is an example of how we can work on ourselves and thereby 'serve the world', by letting go of toxic thoughts and feelings that would otherwise continue to weigh us down. Forgiveness is definitely not about excusing or condoning the wrong or irresponsible actions of others. It's about accepting that these things have happened and that, whether the wrongdoer apologised or whether justice was done in the end, forgiveness means letting go and moving on. If this doesn't happen, we just continue to hurt ourselves.

The Simons, in the book mentioned above, offer a comprehensive explanation of forgiveness as we have here defined it and the varieties of wrongdoing that require it if people are to improve their sense of wellbeing. In terms of getting started, here are a few ideas you can consider offering to the children.

- Make use of some of the techniques we have already looked at for dealing with the anger, frustration and other negative feelings associated with wrongdoing. Review the 'Top tips to deal with worrying' (Chapter 2, p. 42) section as some of those are useful when wishing to forgive.
- Use the time-path techniques (starting p. 122) to give comfort to a 'younger self' who has been wronged, together with the realisation that 'despite what happened, I have survived'.
- If you feel guilty for having done wrong, or for not acting when wrongdoing was done to you, apply the 'justice rationale'. Here, guilt is defined as the intention to do harm followed by the act of harming. By that definition you may not be guilty at all, so you should modify that feeling – or at the very least find another and more suitable word rather than guilt. If on the other hand you feel that you *are* guilty, then consider that a wise judge uses mercy as well as punishment. Try meditating on the idea that you have 'done your time'; you have been punished (or punished yourself) enough and can let go of it now.

Teaching the children to be more assertive (which emphatically does not mean being aggressive) can prove very useful in situations where they are being wronged. Type 'assertiveness for children' into the search engine of an online bookseller and you'll have a wealth of titles to choose from. For your own background information, we recommend Manuel J. Smith's *When I Say No I Feel Guilty* (1975). This is a very readable and thorough book packed with practical advice. For a more spiritual approach to letting go and moving on, try Cheri Huber's *Suffering is Optional* (2000). This also draws together a lot of the threads that we have looked at in *Jumpstart! Wellbeing*.

WORDS OF WISDOM

The two most important days in your life are the day you are born and the day you find out why.

(Mark Twain)

– Do you agree? Do you think there are other days that are just as important?
– Do you think Mark Twain means that we are born for a reason? Give a reason for your answer.
– Ask yourself 'Why do I think I'm here?' Notice what ideas pop into mind.

When I do good, I feel good; when I do bad, I feel bad.

(Abraham Lincoln)

– What do you understand by the word 'good' here?
– Do you feel the same as Abraham Lincoln? (Find out who he was if you don't know.)

Sometimes I go about in pity for myself / And all the while a great wind / Is bearing me across the sky.

(Ojibwa saying)

The Ojibwa are a large group of Native Americans and First Nations living in North America. First Nations refers to the original people of Canada and the Americas.

– What do you think feeling pity for yourself has got to do with 'a great wind' in the sky?
– What do you think the writer means when he says the great wind is 'bearing me across the sky'?
– What does it mean to be self-pitying? What do you think could be done to change that behaviour?

To avoid criticism do nothing, say nothing, be nothing.

(Elbert Hubbard)

- What do you think the writer means? Do you agree with the message?
- Do you think the opposite is true; that if we do something, say something and be something we will be criticised? (Think about what 'something' can mean here.)

Life is too short to be little.

(Benjamin Disraeli)

- What do you think 'little' means here?
- What does a 'big' life mean to you?

Happiness is what we have divided by what we expect.
(Attributed to psychologist Edward Edinger, quoted in Gellert 2007)

- What do you think this quote means?
- Think for a while about what you expect out of life.
- What is the difference between expecting, hoping, wanting, needing and intending?

More quotes can be found in *One Hundred Ways to Serenity* compiled by Celia Haddon (1998).

COMPASSIONATE LIVING

Compassion means 'co-suffering' and is often defined as a feeling of deep sympathy with and sorrow for the suffering of others, combined with a desire to help alleviate that suffering. Stated in these terms it sounds very dramatic and would require a towering act of self-sacrifice to achieve, given the amount of suffering that exists in the world. Indeed many people throughout the ages have lived compassionately to this extent and set the standard of sensitivity, concern and fellow feeling that the rest of us might aspire to.

Truly speaking, compassion is not the same as altruism or empathy, though it is connected. Altruism is an action that brings benefit to others, though we may have little or no emotional involvement in being altruistic. Empathy is an 'emotional mirroring' of another's feelings, though it may involve an act on our part to alleviate those feelings, given that they cause suffering. We might say that compassion brings together the most beneficial elements of altruism and empathy.

Various research studies have indicated that compassion is instinctive in both humans and some animals. If so then we all have the capacity to alleviate suffering, even in small ways as part of our day-to-day lives. Kindness, caring and a willingness to help are the indicators of our compassionate nature. Further studies suggest that acts of compassion help us to form a sense of meaning and purpose in our lives, while some researchers believe that living compassionately has a positive influence on our physical health and on our mental and emotional wellbeing (reference: www. psychologicalscience.org/index.php/publications/observer/ 2013/may-june-13/the-compassionate-mind.html).

It's important to realise however that acts of compassion are not made *because* we want to benefit in these ways. Compassion is about giving something for its own sake without the expectation of reward. The fact that trying to live compassionately does bring benefits to us is a bonus.

- Explain the nature of compassion to the children and ask them to reflect on any occasions they can remember when they have helped someone in this way and when others have helped them.
- Consider launching a class project focusing on people whose acts of compassion are a source of inspiration to us all, such as Mother Teresa, Martin Luther King, Jr., and Desmond Tutu.
- Ask children to imagine that they are wearing 'compassion glasses' for a while. These can be purely imaginary or, better still, actual spectacle frames if you can get them, or ones the children can make from card. When children put these on they try to see the world through compassionate eyes. Asking themselves, 'How does he or she feel?' and 'What can I do to help?'

- Create the opportunity for children to compile a 'compassion journal'. This could be done individually or the journal could be a class project. It would contain news clippings, appropriate quotes and written entries from the children about things they have done to help others.
- Some evolutionary biologists argue that 'the compassion instinct' evolved to help bind communities socially and emotionally, which in turn allows the rearing of the greatest number of offspring. This mechanistic view may well be true, but you might also want children to ponder whether a person is 'more than the sum of the parts'; whether there is more to each of us than a body and a mind (however you define that!).

We have deliberately given this book a practical and secular focus, though some of the material we have presented has been drawn from various spiritual traditions. If you wish to take your wellbeing programme in that direction then we believe you will find that exploring the spiritual aspects of our natures (not necessarily with any reference to organised religion) will add further depth to the ideas we have presented and help children to understand why our species is often called human-kind.

Afterword

In her book *The Great Takeover: how materialism, the media and markets now dominate our lives* (Craig 2012), author Carol Craig (Chief Executive of the Centre for Confidence and Wellbeing) quotes a study by UNICEF into the wellbeing of children in 20 rich nations. Those in the UK scored lowest, just behind the USA. Craig notes seven measures of wellbeing (or the absence of it) as it relates to children and young adults, and asserts that all have risen dramatically in the UK in the past few decades. These measures are: depression, anxiety, obesity, self-harm, eating disorders, conduct problems and ADHD (attention deficit hyperactivity disorder). Craig wonders whether, given poorer countries had a higher placing in the UNICEF study, values, way of life or culture must play a part.

Jumpstart! Wellbeing is not a political polemic but, like Carol Craig, we are alarmed to think that children and young adults seem to be facing more difficulties, as noted above, than ever before. While attempting to change a culture is like trying to turn an ocean liner by pushing it from a rowboat, it is eminently possible for individuals to change the way they think and feel about themselves and the society they live in.

That has been our primary aim in this book, to offer some practical ideas for establishing wellbeing strategies in your classroom to help people to change, and to point the way towards further resources. Having said this, while many of the techniques we offer are quick and easy to apply, we do not for a moment underestimate how demanding it can be for people faced with difficulties of whatever kind to improve the sense of satisfaction, fulfilment and meaningfulness in their lives.

Sometimes to achieve this requires a huge shift of worldview, challenging beliefs and attitudes that may be deeply embedded in a person's sense of self. It may mean a thorough reassessment of basic values about what we want or need out of life; about what life means or should mean to each of us as we journey through an all-too-brief span of years.

Developing a raised sense of wellbeing is also about feeling more comfortable with ourselves and the experiences we encounter. It is the exact opposite of being gullible, weak minded, 'New Age', mystical, resigned, soft or fatalistic. The same inner strength that wellbeing requires is itself strengthened by practising its techniques, reflecting upon its ethos and acting upon the insights it offers. In this sense wellbeing bootstraps itself to greater heights of effectiveness.

As children work towards and enjoy greater mental and emotional wellbeing they will almost inevitably develop a clearer and sharper sense of meaning and purpose in their lives. This may or may not include a spiritual component, but we think it highly likely it will strengthen their sense of connectedness with other people, the world we live in and the universe at large.

The whole field of wellbeing, and everything we have said in this book, is highlighted dramatically by two quotations, one from Mahatma Gandhi and the other by Etienne de Grellet, a Quaker Missionary...

Be the change you want to see in the world.

I shall pass this way but once; any good that I can do or any kindness I can show to any human being; let me do it now. Let me not defer nor neglect it, for I shall not pass this way again.

Bibliography

Basho, M. (1966) *The Narrow Road to the Deep North and other travel sketches.* London: Penguin.

Bowkett, S. (2009) *Countdown to Creative Writing.* Abingdon, Oxon: Routledge.

Bowkett, S. (2015) *Jumpstart! Thinking Skills and Problem Solving.* Abingdon, Oxon: Routledge.

Bowkett, S. and Percival, S. (2011) *Coaching Emotional Intelligence in the Classroom.* Abingdon, Oxon: Routledge.

Bruce-Mitford, M. (1996) *The Illustrated Book of Signs & Symbols.* London: Dorling Kindersley.

Campbell, J. (1988) *The Power of Myth.* New York: Anchor Books.

Campbell, J. (1994) *The Way of Myth.* Boston, Massachusetts: Shambala.

Carnegie, D. (1971) *How to Win Friends and Influence People.* Tadworth, Surrey: World's Work.

Carnegie, D. (1972) *How to Stop Worrying and Start Living.* Tadworth, Surrey: World's Work.

Claxton. (2002) *Building Learning Power.* Bristol: TLO Limited.

Claxton, Chambers, Powell and Lucas. (2011) *The learning Powered School.* Bristol: TLO Limited.

Craig, C. (2012) *The Great Takeover: how materialism, the media and markets now dominate our lives.* Glendaruel, Argyll: Argyll Publishing. [www.centreforconfidence.co.uk/index.php See also http://tedxtalks.ted.com and search for Carol Craig.]

Department for Education (2012a) *The Impact of Pupil Behaviour and Wellbeing on Educational Outcomes.* Department for Education. Research Report DFE-RR253. [www.gov.uk/government/uploads/system/uploads/attachment_data/file/219638/DFE-RR253.pdf]

Department for Education (2012b) *The Impact of Pupil Behaviour and Wellbeing on Educational Outcomes*. Department for Education. Research Brief DFE-RB253. [www.gov.uk/government/uploads/system/uploads/attachment_data/file/197650/DFE-RB253.pdf]

Department for Education (2016) *Mental Health and Behaviour in Schools: departmental advice for school staff*. [www.gov.uk/government/uploads/system/uploads/attachment_data/file/326551/Mental_Health_and_Behaviour_-_Information_and_Tools_for_Schools_final_website__2__25-06-14.pdf]

Ellis, A. (2006) *How To Stubbornly Refuse To Make Yourself Miserable About Anything – Yes, Anything*. Kindle edition.

Fontana & Slack. (1977) *Teaching Meditation to Children*. Element.

Gardner, W. H. (Ed.) (1970) *Gerard Manley Hopkins: poems and prose*. Harmondworth, Middlesex: Penguin. Reference, poem 34, 'As kingfishers catch fire, dragonflies draw flame.'

Gellert, M. (2007) *The Way of the Small: why less is truly more*. Kindle edition.

Goleman, D. (2004) *Emotional Intelligence*. London: Bloomsbury.

Haddon, C. (1998) *One Hundred Ways to Serenity*. London: Hodder & Stoughton.

Hanh, Thich Nhat (1993) *Present Moment, Wonderful Moment: mindfulness verses for daily living*. London: Rider Press.

Hill, N. and Stone, W. Clement (1984) *Success Through a Positive Mental Attitude*. Wellingborough, Northants: Thorsons.

Hirsh-Pasek, K. and Golinkoff, R. M. (2004) *Einstein Never Used Flash Cards: how children really learn – and why they need to play more and memorize less*. Emmaus: Rodale Books.

Honoré, C. (2004) *In Praise of Slow*. London: Orion.

House of Commons Education Committee (2015) *Life Lessons: PSHE and SRE in schools*. Fifth Report of Session 2014–15. [www.publications.parliament.uk/pa/cm201415/cmselect/cmeduc/145/145.pdf]

Huber, C. (2000) *Suffering is Optional*. [www.keepitsimplebooks.com]

Kabat-Zinn, J. (1990) *Full Catastrophe Living*. London: Piatkus.

Kabat-Zinn, J. (2001) *Mindfulness Meditation for Everyday Life*. London: Piatkus.

Kabat-Zinn, J. (2009) *Letting Everything Become Your Teacher*. New York: Bantam Dell.

McGrath, C. (2014) – *The Peer Massage Project*. The Website .http://peermassageproject.co.uk/

Meek, M. (1998) *On Being Literate*. London: The Bodley Head.

Propp, V. (2001) *Morphology of the Folktale*. Austin, Texas: University of Texas Press.

Simon, S. B. and Simon, S. (1991) *Forgiveness: how to make peace with your past and get on with your life*. New York: Warner Books.

Smith, A. (1998) *Accelerated Learning in Practice: brain-based methods for accelerating motivation and achievement*. Stafford: Network Educational Press.

Smith, M. J. (1975) *When I Say No I Feel Guilty*. New York: Bantam Books.

Statham, J. and Chase, E. (2010) *Childhood Wellbeing: a brief overview*. Childhood Wellbeing Research Centre. [www.gov.uk/government/uploads/system/uploads/attachment_data/file/183197/Child-Wellbeing-Brief.pdf]

Stock, G. (1987) *The Book of Questions*. Wellingborough, Northants: Equation.

Stock, G (2004) *The Kids' Book of Questions*. New York: The Workman Publishing Company.

Tolle, E. (2005) *The Power of Now*. London: Hodder & Stoughton.

Wilson, R. A. (1999) *The New Inquisition*. Phoenix, Arizona: New Falcon Publications.

Young, E. (2002) '"Hidden tree" the secret of Zen garden.' *New Scientist*, Daily News, 25 September. [www.newscientist.com/article/dn2838-hidden-tree-the-secret-of-zen-garden/]

Get ready to...

Jumpstart!

The *Jumpstart!* books contain 'quick-figure' ideas that could be used as warm-ups and starters as well as possibly extended into lessons. There are more than 50 games and activities for Key Stage 1 or 2 classrooms that are practical, easy-to-do and vastly entertaining.

To find out more about other books in the Jumpstart! series, or to order online, please visit:

www.routledge.com/u/jumpstart/

Printed in Great Britain
by Amazon